UNLESS SOMEONE TELLS THEM

Forty Days to Better Understand and Communicate God's Eternal Truth

Dr. Ron Harris

Unless Someone Tells Them:
Forty Days to Better Understand and Communicate God's Eternal Truth
ISBN: 9798306099682
Copyright © Ronald L. Harris

All rights reserved. No part of this publication may be reproduced, distributed or transmitted in any form or by any means, including photocopying, recording, or other electronic or mechanical methods, without the prior written permission of the publisher.

Unless otherwise indicated, all Scripture quotations are taken from the Holy Bible, New Living Translation, copyright © 1996, 2004, 2015 by Tyndale House Foundation. Used by permission of Tyndale House Publishers, Carol Stream, Illinois 60188. All rights reserved.

Printed in the United States of America

MEDIA Alliance Publishing
PO Box 200552, Arlington, TX 76006
mediaalliance.net
2024 – 1st edition

Cover and Layout Design: Kyle Gilbert
Author Photo: David Edmonson

Contents

Introduction 5
Who stands fast? 9
The ripple effect 12
I hurried right past the words 15
Where are today's big miracles? 19
Spinning my wheels 23
Are you talking to me? 27
So, you want to be a leader 30
A VIP...Very Influential Person 33
Do you understand? 36
What's that in your hand? 41
How's your big toe? 45
Who are you? 49
On a scale of 1 to 10 53
How many do you see? 57
Prayer. Is it on your To-Do list? 60
How far can you see? 63
What are you willing to do? 67
Things not worth doing 70
Were the "good old days" really good? 75

Distractions...I've had a few	79
A string and two cans	84
What lasts?	89
That's impossible!	93
Turn on the power	96
Don't out-think yourself	100
The Medium is the Message	105
Success! Now what?	110
The world's best tutor	113
Check your ego	117
Cynicism? Yeah...sure!	121
Too Good to be True?	125
Ready or not	128
Why settle for less?	132
What are you known for?	136
Bible Quiz time	139
Light...or life?	142
He maketh me to lie down	146
That pesky law of Newton's	149
Is there an uncomfortable zone?	152
What matters to you?	156

Introduction

What does it take to share God's Good News with others? Many of us have gone through programs that teach us methods to present the Gospel, yet few of us consistently follow through to witness. There is a hurting world that needs hope and salvation.

Yes, it takes some boldness to begin a conversation with someone about their eternal destination. But rather than a programmed way of sharing the Gospel, I believe it best comes out of the overflow of a life that is committed daily to growing deeper with Jesus. Then, we can simply communicate what the Lord is doing in our lives with those around us.

Communication. It's not just an academic college course. It isn't a high and lofty philosophical process. It is how people, including you and me, share thoughts. A father and mother communicate to their children. Instructions. Love. Direction. Truth. And it is how God imparts His Truth to us, with your active participation.

True communication happens when there is a speaker, a message, and someone who receives the message. MEDIA

Alliance is privileged to work with Christian media leaders to strengthen that communication process so that more people—those lost without the hope of the Lord in their lives—can receive the Word and come to know Jesus as their Savior.

Over the life of the MEDIA Alliance ministry, we have shared weekly insights on communication, leadership, media, and personal spiritual growth. God's Word compels us. Paul told the Romans we have a great responsibility to share the hope of the Lord.

> *But how can they call on him to save them unless they believe in him? And how can they believe in him if they have never heard about him? And how can they hear about him unless someone tells them?*
>
> ROMANS 10:14 NLT

In this book, we have gleaned a few of the weekly blogs from the over 500 we've penned through the years for this forty-day devotional to strengthen you in your spiritual journey and to prepare you to communicate God's hope to those right around you. I pray that our Lord will speak to your heart and give you the boldness to be His great communicator of His great Truth.

Ron Harris
MEDIA Alliance International

DAY ONE

Who stands fast?

Life-long learner. That's what I try to be. And I have so much to learn! Sometimes I feel that the smartphone in my pocket is secretly laughing at me! That phone and other ever-changing technologies compel me to be that life-long learner, whether I want to or not. I know I can't learn everything, but my life can be greatly enriched and inspired as I gain knowledge and, hopefully, some wisdom.

One of my privileges is working with media leaders and faithful Christ-followers in over forty-five countries. Each person in each country and culture enriches my life. In fact, many are my heroes, and I learn much from them.

So many of them serve in hard places, facing government challenges and cultural pushback for their work in Christian media. Yet they stand fast. These dedicated leaders are teaching many of us what it means to stay committed to the cause of Christ, even in the face of adversity.

German theologian Dietrich Bonhoeffer was one who stood his ground against great odds, and it ultimately cost Bonhoeffer his life. Prior to his death, this Christian leader who stood strong in the midst of overwhelming moral compromise in his land wrote this:

> "Who stands fast? Only the man whose final standard is not his reason, his principles, his conscience, his freedom, or his virtue, but who is ready to sacrifice all this when he is called to obedient and responsible action in faith and in exclusive allegiance to God—the responsible man, who tries to make his whole life an answer to the question and call of God. Where are these responsible people?"

A good question. Where are these responsible people today? Yes, Bonhoeffer's stand on his allegiance to Christ resulted in his tragic death. But Dietrich Bonhoeffer understood that God changes tribulation to glory. He believed, as the Apostle Paul, who told the Christ-followers in Colossae:

> *We pray that you'll live well for the Master, making him proud of you as you work hard in his orchard. As you learn more and more how God works, you will learn how to do your work. We pray that you'll have the strength to stick*

it out over the long haul—not the grim strength of gritting your teeth but the glory-strength God gives. It is strength that endures the unendurable and spills over into joy, thanking the Father who makes us strong enough to take part in everything bright and beautiful that he has for us.

Colossians 1:11 MSG

Strength that endures the unendurable...and spills over into joy. That is quite a challenge...and quite a calling. May our life-long learning surpass just the technical or the interesting things of life. May it focus more on learning how to serve our Lord Jesus, proclaiming His Name and His hope to a lost and hopeless world, and do it with great joy. Our example is Jesus...

...the champion who initiates and perfects our faith. Because of the joy awaiting him, he endured the cross, disregarding its shame. Now he is seated in the place of honor beside God's throne.

Hebrews 12:2 NLT

May our Heavenly Father count each of us among those who stand fast.

DAY TWO

The ripple effect...

Do you ever catch yourself saying something your father said? At the time you heard it, you may have rolled your eyes, shrugged, and vowed never to say anything like that to anyone. Yet, here you are, being influenced by others, and it is rippling through you.

Fred Smith was a wise man. He was an influencer. Fred has been quoted as saying, "We each ripple the pond of human life. Some make dainty circles, while others make big splashes. Yet the movement of the water continues."

Our influence lives on...for good or bad.

Have you felt the influence of others? Parents? Teachers who poured themselves into the students...into you? A coach, a pastor, or a church leader? They have helped shape you and mold you into who you are today. And there are those today looking to you to learn, to grow, to be influenced by you and your life—

personally, professionally, and spiritually.

Here are some things to consider and some questions to ask as you think about influence:

- Who is currently influencing me?
- What influence am I exerting in my family, at work, and in the community?
- How can I choose positive influencers?

Words of wisdom to remember: "Influence never dies."

From the Old Testament to the New Testament, God's Word directs us to be influencers for the glory of our God.

Obey them [God's statutes] completely, and you will display your wisdom and intelligence among the surrounding nations. When they hear all these decrees, they will exclaim, 'How wise and prudent are the people of this great nation!'

Deuteronomy 4:6 NLT

The Apostle Paul's letters to his young mentee Timothy repeatedly show how Paul, influenced by Jesus himself, was rippling God's influence on Timothy.

> *Timothy, my son, here are my instructions for you.... May they help you fight well in the Lord's battles. Cling to your faith in Christ, and keep your conscience clear.*
>
> 1 TIMOTHY 1 18-19 NLT

You are going to influence those around you. The question is, what kind of influencer will you be? What will be the "ripple effect" of your life?

DAY THREE

I hurried right past the words...

In my morning devotional reading, I read right past some words. Two sentences later, I had to go back. I'm sure it was God's Spirit hitting the brakes for me, shifting me in reverse. So, I read the words again.

The Spirit of God...lives within you.

ROMANS 8:1

I had to stop. And think. And sit in wonder at that truth. The great God who fashioned the universe, who put everything in place, who started our world spinning and has interacted throughout history, culminating in sending His Son Jesus to live, die, and be resurrected from the dead—that God lives within me!

Amazing. But understanding that truth led me to ask myself, "What difference does that make? What difference *will* it make today?"

As I communicate the hope of the Gospel to others, do I do that in my own wisdom, or in the wisdom of the One who lives within me? As I lead others in ministry, as I have opportunity to encourage and strengthen the work of others who are impacting the world with God's Truth, do I do so with my good ideas or with God's direction?

God's word through Isaiah to His people clearly defined the Lord's role in our lives:

I am the Lord your God,
who teaches you what is good for you
and leads you along the paths you should follow.

Isaiah 48:17 NLT

Do we believe that? Do we live that? Do we follow that? Paul seems to be in awe and wonder as he writes his thoughts on God's amazing wisdom.

Oh, how great are God's riches and wisdom and knowledge! How impossible it is for us to understand his decisions and his ways!

For who can know the Lord's thoughts?
Who knows enough to give him advice?

ROMANS 11:33-34 NLT

Peter Drucker was arguably the leading management thinker of the 20th century. Many believe his great insight was built upon his faith in God. Drucker is quoted as writing:

> "The personal will of God is a 'bond above them, with the common ruling power, which encompasses everyone everywhere.'"

In other words, God's wisdom should be the overarching truth that is the foundation upon which we build our leadership and our lives. And to think, this wisdom is dwelling within us at all times. God Himself lives within you!

What is the reward for recognizing that fact? Job said it well:

But he knows where I am going.
And when he tests me, I will come out as pure as gold.
For I have stayed on God's paths;

I have followed his ways and not turned aside.
I have not departed from his commands,
but have treasured his words more than daily food.

JOB 23:10-12 NLT

Listen to God's Voice. Treasure His Words. He is right there, living within you!

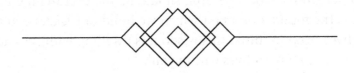

DAY FOUR

Where are today's big miracles?

When Solomon finished praying, fire flashed down from heaven and burned up the burnt offerings and sacrifices, and the glorious presence of the Lord filled the Temple. The priests could not enter the Temple of the Lord because the glorious presence of the Lord filled it.

2 CHRONICLES 7: 1-2 NLT

I came across this passage in my early morning Bible reading and wondered: What would it have been like to be there when this miracle happened? The fire from heaven. The visible presence of the Lord. The awe and wonder at His glorious presence. And then I thought...

Where are today's big miracles?

Why don't we see these things today?

That started me on a brief journey on the subject of miracles. Pastor John Piper says that there were fewer miracles in the Bible than we probably think. And he points out they had very specific purposes...to point people to God.

Piper also says that there are probably more miracles going on around us today than we probably understand. The stories of God at work around the world, through the lives of missionaries, in lands hostile to the Gospel, in dire situations in our land or yours...if all were known, we would likely be awed by the hand of God showing Himself in a miraculous way.

The reality is that most of the people of the Bible did not see great miracles, but they learned of them through the telling and retelling of God's faithfulness. Jesus performed miracles to verify his authority as God's Son. He gave His disciples the ability to do miraculous things so that the people could see and comprehend the fulfillment of God's salvation through His Son, Jesus.

Even then, Jesus didn't heal everyone. Nor did His disciples. Jesus raised three people from the dead, but many he did not. There were those around Jesus who suffered and died without a miracle in their lives. Even His disciples suffered for their faith, most dying painful deaths at the hands of Christ's enemies.

If Jesus Christ is the same yesterday, today, and tomorrow—and He is—we shouldn't need to see the big miracles to live out our faith. We can trust God for His ability to do His work in our lives and then look forward with hope for the future.

Miracles today? We all have probably seen a life changed by the power of God's Holy Spirit and we can only say it is a miracle of the Lord. Some people receive miraculous reports from the doctors that they are healed or that cancer previously detected is now gone. A modern-day miracle. But that doesn't happen in every case. The fact that God even answers prayer is a miracle when we realize that the great God of the universe doesn't owe us anything.

It may also be that we aren't looking for God's miracles today. Ultimately, though, we need to remember that God is Sovereign. His will determines if something miraculous happens, and it is for His purpose, not our personal experience.

Of course, our own salvation is a miracle of God. He has no reason to save me except by his miraculous grace. And that is a miracle we should tell over and over so that others might come to know our Lord Jesus. Then we would experience another miracle—another life changed by Christ Jesus.

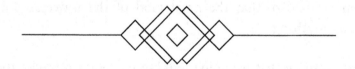

DAY FIVE

Spinning my wheels...

When Judy and I got married almost sixty years ago, we honeymooned near the Texas Gulf Coast. And as we started for home, I wanted to do what my family had often done on trips to Galveston and the Bolivar Peninsula. We pulled off the highway to cross a path through some small sand dunes to get to the beach. We wanted to spend some time walking along the beach, hand in hand, listening to the sound of the surf and the gulls as they flew overhead. Sounds romantic, right?

It would have been except for one thing: the sand dunes. My car got bogged down in the soft, dry sand, and I couldn't move forward or backward. I tried to dig out the sand from around the wheels with my hands. The wheels were just spinning! I was stuck.

Eventually, someone in a truck passed by who had a chain, and he was able to pull and jerk my dad's 1965 Chevrolet and get us onto solid ground. I was thankful for a rather good ending to this sad but true story.

I must confess, there have been other times in my life when I felt frustrated and like I was spinning my wheels. No matter what I tried, the end results were not good. Maybe you have felt that frustration, too.

In the book of Haggai, the Lord addressed His people with an explanation of some of their "wheel spinning" situations. Listen.

> *Look at what's happening to you! You have planted much but harvested little. You eat but are not satisfied. You drink but are still thirsty. You put on clothes but cannot keep warm. Your wages disappear as though you were putting them in pockets filled with holes!*
>
> HAGGAI 1:5-6 NLT

The Lord explained through Haggai what was going on and why His people were having so much trouble. They had been putting themselves and their comfort and prosperity above the Lord. Earlier, God quoted what the Israelites had been saying. "The time has not yet come to rebuild the house of the Lord." (v.2). Yet, He said they were living in luxury, and His house was in ruins. I wonder how often we have neglected the important things of the Lord in order to be comfortable. I wonder how many times we have overlooked God's will and God's way so that we might fulfill our own ideas. Have I put myself and my plans above those of the Lord? Have I said, in effect, "Lord, I have a better idea. I'll get around to You and Your way later."

Listen to God's Word:

> *Commit everything you do to the Lord. Trust him, and he will help you.*
>
> PSALM 37:5 NLT

> *Commit your actions to the Lord, and your plans will succeed.*
>
> PROVERBS 16:3 NLT

> *Trust in the Lord with all your heart; do not depend on your own understanding.*
> *Seek his will in all you do, and he will show you which path to take.*
>
> PROVERBS 3:5-6 NLT

A bit later in Haggai, we see God's promise to His people when they decided to put Him first, and they began work on the temple.

> *I am giving you a promise now while the seed is still in the barn. You have not yet harvested your grain, and your grapevines, fig trees, pomegranates, and olive trees have not yet produced their crops. But from this day onward I will bless you.*
>
> HAGGAI 2:19 NLT

Let's stop spinning our wheels. Let's be sure we are putting the Lord and His ways, His plans, first. And then, let's see what happens in our lives and our ministries as the Lord keeps His promises to us.

DAY SIX
Are you talking to me?

Do you ever wonder if God is speaking to you? I mean, directly?

A while back, I recorded a promo for a new sermon series by my pastor. The series was called "Invincible," and the promo began like this:

> "What is your Everest? That mountain you keep coming to that seems insurmountable?"

Then I picked up a book by Mark Batterson titled *Chase the Lion*. The theme is based on a brief passage about a man who became one of King David's mighty warriors. His name is Benaiah. Have you heard of him? I didn't recognize the name but later found him in a listing of some of David's most valiant warriors. Batterson, a pastor in Washington, D.C., has built a philosophy of life around that short scripture. Here is the passage:

On a snowy day, he chased a lion down into a pit and killed it.

2 Samuel 23:20 NLT

I had to look that up. I know I have read through the Bible multiple times and the books of Samuel, but this passage has never caught my eye—until now.

Batterson says that chasing a lion into a pit on a snowy day is not a normal action. That's an understatement! It is probably the exact opposite of what I would do. Are you with me on that? I hope to never be in a position to have to find out how I would deal with that exact situation.

Benaiah's display of courage seemed to set the pattern for the warrior's life, ultimately propelling him to a high position in David's army. Batterson says that "chase the lion" is more than a catchy phrase.

"Most of us spend our lives running away from things we are afraid of. We forfeit our dreams on the altar of fear. Or we chase after the wrong things."

So, what is your "Everest?" is there something before you that is holding you back from doing what you believe God wants you to accomplish? Is something keeping you from being who the Lord has called you to be?

Mark Batterson has gone so far as to write a "Lion Chaser's Manifesto" to challenge and encourage those facing challenges. After talking about going after our dreams and facing our giants to accomplish God's purpose, Batterson adds this admonition:

> Quit living as if the purpose of life is to arrive safely at death.

Have you figured out what keeps you from that "one thing" God has for you? That Everest? That lion that seems to be in your way? The Apostle Paul said he was pressing on, despite the past or the challenges of the day, "for the high calling of God in Christ Jesus."

That's a good goal for us, too.

DAY SEVEN

So, you want to be a leader...

First, let's get something straight. We are all leaders—to one degree or another. It may be in our homes or among our friends. It may be that the Lord has placed us in areas of leadership in ministry. And if we are honest with ourselves, we sometimes feel inadequate to be in that role. Very few of us have a degree in leadership. However, many of us desire to be the leaders that God has called us to be.

Of all the leadership books out there—and there are a zillion of them—the best ones for me are those based on the principles found in God's Word and based on amazing biblical leaders. *Spiritual Leadership* by Henry and Richard Blackaby comes to mind, along with *Lead Like Jesus* by Ken Blanchard and Phil Hodges.

Having said that, there are many things to learn from those who have researched leaders and leadership. Many of us have gained from studies by Jim Collins in his classic book *Good to Great*. These examples help us identify traits that successful leaders have and allow us to analyze our leadership style to see where we can improve.

When the Lord moves us into leadership roles, it is not to build us up. It is to build up His work to accomplish His purpose. And He doesn't move us into leadership to fail. If we learn from His Word and give attention to our own hearts and attitudes toward others, we can become extraordinary leaders who accomplish much for God and His Kingdom.

I boil my leadership guide down to four words.

Love God. Love people.

My basis for this is from Jesus, who, when asked what the greatest commandment was, responded this way:

> *"'You must love the Lord your God with all your heart, all your soul, and all your mind.' This is the first and greatest commandment. A second is equally important: 'Love your*

neighbor as yourself.'"

MATTHEW 22:37-39 NLT

Many are looking at you, at your life, at your priorities. May they see the godly principles the Lord gives to all He calls.

Lead on...

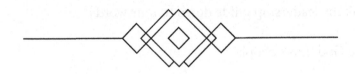

DAY EIGHT

A VIP...Very Influential Person

I've got some good news! For those of us who often feel we aren't the smartest person in the room, we can still be a person of real and lasting influence. Whether it is our kids, our staff, or our circle of friends we want to influence, most of us would like to have a positive effect on these people and influence them for God and for good.

Dr. Richard Blackaby recently wrote about being a person of influence, sharing some important points and some examples from the life of his father and my spiritual mentor, Dr. Henry Blackaby. "My father, Henry, was a shy, introverted Canadian. But God used him to exert enormous influence on others."

People often sought out the godly wisdom Dr. Henry Blackaby shared, and with that wisdom came great influence. I was one among many who asked for guidance from this man who, though shy and certainly with his flaws, spoke wisdom into the hearts of kings, presidents, and top CEOs. A man of influence.

What does it take to have such an impact? Richard Blackaby lists these items as key for a person desiring to have godly influence.

- Have something of value to say. - How do you become someone who has something to say? Study. Think. Prepare. Too many people want the prestige of influence without paying the price to earn it.
- Refrain from speaking when you have nothing of value to contribute. - The author of Proverbs sagely declares, "Even a fool is counted wise when he holds his peace; When he shuts his lips, he is considered perceptive." (Prov. 17:28 NKJV).
- Always tell the truth, regardless of how unpopular. - Sadly, in today's politically correct climate, people frequently say things that are patently untrue but politically correct. If you always tell the truth, you may not always be popular, but your opinions will carry weight.
- Be discerning. - Influential people have an uncanny sense of timing. Jesus warned His followers to beware

of casting pearls before swine (Matt. 7:6). Better to wait until the time is ripe and the audience is open.

- Be Spirit-led. - The apostle Paul exhorted, "See then that you walk circumspectly, not as fools but as wise, redeeming the time, because the days are evil. Therefore, do not be unwise, but understand what the will of the Lord is. And do not be drunk with wine, in which is dissipation; but be filled with the Spirit..." (Eph. 5:15-18 NKJV).

Do you want to make an eternal difference in the lives of those around you? God's wisdom outlasts and outperforms anything man may have to offer from a human perspective. Share His wisdom, and you will find that your life has a greater influence than you thought ever possible.

DAY NINE
Do you understand?

Let me be honest with you. I don't understand. A lot.

In my Old Testament Bible readings, I see the way the children of Israel watch God do amazing, miraculous things...and then turn around and complain...or make idols to worship instead of the God who had delivered them and provided for them. I don't understand.

I read Peter saying he would never deny Jesus...would even die first...then within hours, he denies the Lord three times...just as Jesus predicted. I don't understand.

In our modern world, I see good friends, healthy friends who have served their Lord Jesus for decades, contract the COVID-19 virus and within days are dead, while others seem to slide through the virus with little or no symptoms. I don't understand.

Judy and I have had our share of troubles in past years. Sometimes, I have to admit I don't understand why she has had to endure multiple surgeries and hospital stays.

I don't understand.

But I guess I am in somewhat good company. David often questioned God about why the enemy seemed to have the upper hand or why God didn't seem to answer.

> *My God, my God, why have you abandoned me? Why are you so far away when I groan for help? Every day I call to you, my God, but you do not answer. Every night I lift my voice, but I find no relief.*
>
> PSALM 22:1-2 NLT

David could have added… "I don't understand."

And the prophet Habakkuk also struggled to understand why things were happening in his culture, why the enemy seemed to be winning all the battles.

> *How long, O Lord, must I call for help? But you do not*

listen! "Violence is everywhere!"
I cry, but you do not come to save. Must I forever see these evil deeds?

Habakkuk 1: 2-3 NLT

Habakkuk goes on and on with his complaint. He also could easily have added, "I don't understand."

But here is a bulletin:

God doesn't owe us any explanation.

He has often said, "My ways are not your ways." And He has reminded us that He is a Sovereign God. He can bless whomever He wants to bless and curse whomever He wants to curse. He is God Almighty over all.

So, what do we do? Just hunker down and endure? Not exactly.

We should follow the example of David and Habakkuk, among others. Later in Psalm 22 David acknowledges the holiness of the Lord and follows with this direction for his own life.

> *I will proclaim your name to my brothers and sisters, I will praise you among your assembled people. Praise the Lord.... Honor Him...Show him reverence...*
>
> Psalm 22: 22-23, 25 NLT

And one of the most beautiful canticles of praise in the whole Bible came from Habakkuk after he had complained to the Lord. In it, the prophet says that if the whole world falls apart, "...yet, I will rejoice in the Lord! I will be joyful in the God of my salvation! The Sovereign Lord is my strength!" (Habakkuk 3:18-19 NLT)

The old hymn writers got it right.

> Trials dark on every hand,
> And we cannot understand,
> All the ways that God would lead us
> To that blessed Promised Land.
> But He guides us with His eye
> And we'll follow till we die.
> For we'll understand it better by and by.

In these days when we do not—cannot—understand what God is doing or why He is allowing all that is swirling around us, we must simply trust the heart of an all-loving God. He is Sovereign. And—He does understand!

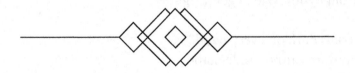

DAY TEN
What's that in your hand?

There is a credit card company that uses famous actors to extol the wonderful virtues of using their card. Their now-famous line at the end of the commercials is, "What's in your wallet?" In other words, with their credit card in your wallet, you have great spending power, and all your cares are over...until the bill comes in the mail!

In a higher (and holier) way, God says to us... "What's in your hand?"

Many of us learned during those days of stay-at-home edicts and pandemic crisis that we can do without a lot of things we thought we needed. We often approach the task and ministry to which the Lord has called us by saying, "If I only had this tool," or "If I had that set of folks on my team," thinking this is what is needed to do what God has enlisted us to do.

Reading through the Bible, a practice of mine for over ten years, has recently taken me back through Exodus. We find the amazing story of Moses, who was in great favor with the Egyptian royalty, then out of favor and exiled to the back side of the wilderness, tending flocks. Until God spoke to him.

Do you remember the encounter? The bush in the wilderness was burning, but it wasn't burning up. Just burning. Moses said to himself, "I have got to see this amazing sight." Of course, when he arrived, he found himself on holy ground with the great God of the universe speaking directly to him. Moses was shocked and overwhelmed. Who wouldn't be? But that feeling led Moses to express himself to God in a way that angered the Lord.

"Who am I?"

A number of years ago I was on the verge of being named to a key position. It was a position of honor, but it was overwhelming to me. So much so that I called my spiritual mentor, Dr. Henry Blackaby, and explained my situation. And I quoted Moses at that point. "Who am I?" I should have remembered that was not a high spiritual moment for Moses. Dr. Blackaby did remember, and he gently said to me, "Ron, you shouldn't be saying, 'Who am I?' You should be saying, 'Who is God?'" And he was absolutely right.

As I recently reread that encounter between God and Moses, I was struck by that phrase the Lord uttered to Moses as he was trying to explain his mission and how it would be accomplished.

"What is that in your hand?"

Exodus 4:2 NLT

Moses was trying to figure out how it was all going to work. God wanted Moses to simply commit and obey. What Moses had in his hand was what he had been using for those forty years to herd sheep and goats. A shepherd's staff. A rod. A big stick. But God had a formula for success that went way beyond Moses' understanding. Here it is.

God + You + Your Obedience = Success

The Lord then began to show Moses how it was going to work. If Moses would be obedient, be willing to use what was already in his hand and follow God's direction, Moses would be successful in rescuing the children of Israel from the oppression of the people of Egypt.

Today, we have a world living under sin's oppression. What will it take to successfully show them there is freedom in Christ? What is in your hand? What has the Lord already provided you in the way of skills, opportunities, wisdom, and passion? Will you be obedient to the Lord as He speaks to your heart? Instead of saying, "Who am I?" or "How can I do this great task?" you should simply say, "Yes, Lord. Use me and whatever I may have in my hand to impact lives with your Truth."

What's in your hand?

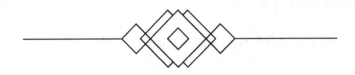

DAY ELEVEN

How's your big toe?

Well, it sure caught my attention. I was reading a devotional by my pastor, Dr. Robert Jeffress, and I read this thought:

"Nobody stubs his toe standing still."

Interesting thought. And what is wrapped around that thought is the idea that mistakes will come. Problems will arise. We will sometimes fail. That "stubbed toe" is a sign that you are moving forward, active, trying to get somewhere.

Suppose you are walking through your house to go to the kitchen for a cup of coffee and you hit your toe on a table leg. Ouch. Been there, done that. There might be some hopping around and grabbing of the painful toe. And then you would probably just limp on into the kitchen to get that cup of coffee.

Imagine, though, that you just sat down on the floor and said to yourself, "That's it. I'm done. I sure won't try that again. I guess

I'll just give up coffee. In fact, I think I'll just carefully retreat to my room and never come out." Crazy. Silly. Yet sometimes, we do similar things when we stumble in our ministries and in our lives.

As others have said, failure isn't final. That is such good news. And it isn't just positive thinking; it's the truth from the Lord Jesus.

One of the most poignant passages in scripture has to do with failure. Predicted failure. You remember Peter, who often said things without fully thinking them through, saying to Jesus at the Last Supper, "Lord, you can count on me, even to the point of death." Jesus responded to him with words that had to upset his disciple.

> *"Peter, let me tell you something. Before the rooster crows tomorrow morning, you will deny three times that you even know me."*
>
> Luke 22:34 NLT

Here is the passage that touches me from the events just a few hours after that encounter. Peter had made his way to the courtyard of the high priest where Jesus had been taken by the Jewish guards. Three different people had tried to link Peter to Jesus. Each time, Peter strongly denied he even knew Jesus, the third time in strong language.

> *And immediately, while he was still speaking, the rooster crowed. At that moment the Lord turned and looked at Peter. Suddenly, the Lord's words flashed through Peter's mind: "Before the rooster crows tomorrow morning, you will deny three times that you even know me." And Peter left the courtyard, weeping bitterly.*
>
> Luke 22:60-63 NLT

Denial. Defeat. Failure. I'm sure Peter thought his life and his worth as a disciple of Christ was over. He did far more than just stub his toe. It was a big-time, predicted failure to which he had succumbed.

Yet after Christ's resurrection, Peter found himself on the beach with the Savior, and Jesus made a point of restoring Peter. Three denials. And three times the Lord gave Peter an assignment:

Feed my lambs, take care of my flock, feed my sheep. Peter was restored and set back on the path to God's goal.

Failure is NOT final, not in God's economy. Yes, it may hurt. Yes, there are lessons to be learned. But if our eyes are on the goal... serving Christ at all costs, a little failure should not sideline us for God's purpose. We see the obstacle. We learn to navigate around it or avoid it. But we move on.

If you have stubbed your toe...get over it. Keep your eye on God's goal, and keep moving forward. It's what Jesus wants you to do.

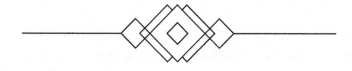

DAY TWELVE

Who are you?

Do you ever get that question? If I asked you to take out a piece of paper and write down in bullet-point form the things that identify you, what would you write? What would be at the top?

Several years ago, I was in a high-level meeting between a pastor of a large church and the head of a major Christian university. After a few minutes of visiting, the head of the university looked at the pastor and said, "Now, who are you?" A rather awkward moment. In his defense, the university president had just come back from vacation and didn't have time to get briefed on who his visitors were.

What would you have said? Most of us would have given our credentials as to our leadership role in a key church in a major city. But would that have been the most important way to identify ourselves?

A recent devotional from *Lead Like Jesus* reminds us of the right perspective we should have as leaders.

> "It can be easy to forget, especially if we hold formal leadership positions, that being a leader is not our identity or calling. We are first children of God, called to follow Jesus."

John Maxwell says, "Leadership is not about titles, positions, or flowcharts. It is about one life influencing another."

It is interesting to read the Facebook profiles of people and see how they describe themselves. Many rightly begin with their relationship with Christ, then go on to list other ways they can be identified. But not everyone does that.

Our identity is important. We need to get it right. Jesus entered into the conversation of some of his disciples who were discussing what others were saying about who Jesus was. Jesus looked at them, Peter in particular, and asked, "But who do *you* say I am?" *(italics added)*

If our identity is bound up in what we do, then we open ourselves up to failure and, often, a spiritual downward spiral. There will be times when we fail when our team fails when we and our good intentions are misunderstood. We need to hide our identity in God's grace, not our own achievements.

In his book *Transforming Grace*, Jerry Bridges gives great insight into this key area for leaders.

> "Living by grace instead of by works means you are free from the performance treadmill. It means God has already given you an "A" when you deserved an "F." ...You are loved and accepted by God through the merit of Jesus... Nothing you ever do will cause Him to love you any more or any less. He loves you strictly by His grace given to you through Jesus."

Let me ask you, what is the overarching identifying trait of your life? Who do your friends say you are? What does your family say when asked about you? What would Jesus say?

The Apostle Paul was well aware of his position. Christ was primary. He was secondary, at best. Eugene Peterson's The Message puts it this way:

I identified myself completely with him (Christ). Indeed, I have been crucified with Christ. My ego is no longer central. It is no longer important that I appear righteous before you or have your good opinion, and I am no longer driven to impress God. Christ lives in me. The life you see me living is not "mine," but it is lived by faith in the Son of God, who loved me and gave himself for me.

GALATIANS 2:19-21 MSG

So, who are you? Most importantly, who does God say you are?

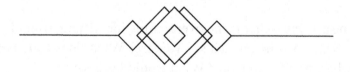

DAY THIRTEEN

On a scale of 1 to 10...

You know that dream you had, that vision for yourself or for your ministry as you serve the Lord? Where is that vision today?

On a scale of 1 to 10, with 1 being still at the starting point and ten being fully realized, where is that dream?

I've had lots of ideas and dreams that never happened. Some remained simply dreams. Others I took down the path, did some preparation and prayer, and never saw the dream come through to fulfillment. I gave up on the dream.

I began working on some ideas until it became obvious they weren't going to happen. Then, a few years later, that vision became reality. It was God's timing that made the difference.

Mark Batterson is well known for some of his great books—The *Circle Maker*, *Draw the Circle*, *In a Pit with a Lion on a Snowy Day*, and others. He is also a lead pastor of a church in Washington, DC. In *Draw the Circle*, he admits, "None of my dreams have ever happened quickly or easily." That kind of takes the wind out of my sails. I often want to go right from having the vision to seeing the vision come about. It rarely happens that way.

Batterson reminds us to keep faith in the One who is always faithful. God will accomplish His will, but it comes in His timing, not ours.

> "Sometimes God will push us to our absolute limits...the limits of our faith, of our patience, of our gifts. That is how God stretches our faith and builds our character."

Dr. Richard Blackaby talks of a crisis of belief that comes to us at critical times in our lives. You have a vision for ministry. You have a dream of establishing something new, reaching new heights, or setting off in new directions. But you get no support, and you feel inadequate to accomplish it on your own. Dr. Blackaby says you must realize that God is God. He can accomplish through you—in His time—what He has put on your heart. Blackaby says don't lose heart. "You have joined a long line of people that God has done amazing things through, but you are going to have to believe Him, and you are going to have to obey Him."

As someone has said, "If you don't get out of the boat, you'll never walk on water." The Israelites would have never left Egypt if they hadn't stepped into the Red Sea. They would never have seen that victory at Jericho if they had stopped circling the walls before the seventh time.

So...where is your dream today? On a scale of 1 to 10, where do you see this vision from God? Have you stopped short in the process of obeying God's vision? Have you given up too soon when the Lord has shown you His plan for your ministry, your life?

It is all about belief in God and obedience to His vision for you, your ministry, and your life. And it is for God's plan and His glory, not about you. Success or failure (by human standards) is not important. Obedience to the Lord is key.

Dr. Henry Blackaby admits that the Lord sometimes asks us to do something beyond our ability to accomplish.

> "Will God ever ask you to do something you are not able to do? The answer is yes—all the time! It must be that way, for God's glory and kingdom. If we function according to our ability alone, we get the glory; if we function according

to the power of the Spirit within us, God gets the glory. He wants to reveal Himself to a watching world."

--Experiencing God Day by Day

Remember, those who have taken the step of faith are watching to see if you will obediently run the race and follow God's vision.

Therefore, since we are surrounded by such a huge crowd of witnesses to the life of faith, let us strip off every weight that slows us down, especially the sin that so easily trips us up. And let us run with endurance the race God has set before us. We do this by keeping our eyes on Jesus, the champion who initiates and perfects our faith....

Hebrews 12:1-2 NLT

If you don't get out of the boat, you'll never walk on water. Take a step, and see God do something miraculous.

DAY FOURTEEN
How many do you see?

All throughout my radio days—now approaching almost sixty years!—I have understood that the best radio engagement is when the presenter understands he/she is speaking to just one person. We call radio a very intimate medium, and that is the reason why.

I grew up in the era of pre-television, when families actually sat around a big console radio and listened to variety programs and radio dramas. Not true today. Our radio and podcast audiences are typically by themselves in a car, or listening on earphones or ear pods on a commuter train, or while jogging in the neighborhood. One person.

While I knew that to be true and have tried to both practice and teach that technique, it was not until recently that I understood it also had biblical foundations. And of all places, it came from a sermon on Jesus and the "wee little man" Zacchaeus. It is a familiar story, especially for little children. You may have already started singing the song:

> Zacchaeus was a wee little man,
> and a wee little man was he.
> He climbed up in the sycamore tree
> for the Lord he wanted to see.

My friend Dr. David Allen preached on the passage in Luke 19 that tells the story. It happened in Jericho on Jesus' way to Jerusalem. Crowds pressed around the roadway, waiting for Jesus to pass. But due to Zacchaeus' size, he had to take radical action to catch a glimpse of Christ. So up the sycamore tree he went.

David Allen's point, which is relevant to us in the media, is this: Jesus doesn't "see" the crowds. He sees the individual. In this case, it was a wee little man. And Jesus called him by name.

Another time, the crowds were pressing in on Jesus when a woman touched the edge of his garment. Immediately, Jesus asked, "Who touched me?" The disciples were incredulous. "The people are all around you, Jesus, pressing in, and you ask, 'Who touched me?'"

Jesus sees the individual and addresses that specific person and their need. We ought to follow that pattern in all our encounters and our sharing of God's hope. Is there a scripture to share? Think of one person and give them that passage. You may be part of God's instructions for life that person needs.

We need to be less concerned with the numbers, the crowd, and more concerned with the solitary person the Lord puts in our path. We need to follow the pattern set by our Savior and think less of the crowd and more of the person who needs a word from the Lord.

How many do you see? The many—or the one?

DAY FIFTEEN

Prayer. Is it on your To-Do list?

When do you pray? How often do you pray? And what kinds of things do you pray about? I'm not trying to probe into your life… but just wanted to get you thinking about the role prayer plays in your daily routine.

At our breakfast table, Judy and I read from a devotional book. In the evening, we read through books of the Bible. A while back a Billy Graham thought on prayer impacted me. He talked about the privilege of prayer and then began to list the times we are to pray.

- We are to pray in times of adversity, lest we become faithless and unbelieving.
- We are to pray in times of prosperity, lest we become boastful and proud.

- We are to pray in times of danger, lest we become fearful and doubting.
- We are to pray in times of security, lest we become self-sufficient.

Wow. It sounds like prayer ought to be our daily priority. In recent years my wife has struggled with multiple health issues, and I have prayed. I have prayed in petition to God. I have prayed thanking God. I have prayed for the Lord's guidance for surgeons. I have later prayed with the surgeons and let them know people around the world were praying. And Judy and I have felt the prayers of our many friends. Prayer is not theoretical, it is our lifeline to the Father.

Oswald Chambers once said, "The only way to get into the relationship of 'asking' is to get into the relationship of absolute reliance on the Lord Jesus." Have you been there? Have you agonized in prayer...and rejoiced in prayer? Chambers also said, "Prayer does not prepare you for the greater work; it is the greater work."

*And we are confident that he hears us
whenever we ask for anything that pleases him.*

1 JOHN 5:14 NLT

We need to pray more, not less, according to His will, with confidence in the One who hears and answers our prayers. Let prayer be your greatest work today.

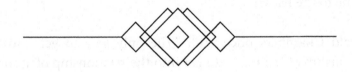

DAY SIXTEEN

How far can you see?

I was looking at computers and printers the other day and noticed the tag phrase for the Epson brand.

Exceed Your Vision

That started me down a thought path. Exceed your vision. See farther than you can see. What does that mean? I thought of the "flat earth" people who only see to the horizon and deduce the earth is flat. (My international air travel tells me differently.)

What does it take to exceed your vision? First, it takes faith. You have to believe there is something "out there" that you can't see—yet. Something that will carry you farther along life's path. From a biblical standpoint, it means trusting in a God who is already out there, seeing the beginning from the end. As the Lord revealed to Isaiah,

Only I can tell you the future before it even happens...

Isaiah 46:10a NLT

In practical terms, what does that phrase mean today for you and for those you may lead? It should be a revolutionary thought that removes the man-made boundaries to what God is calling you to do and to be.

Exceed your vision...

We are sometimes asked, "If money were no object, what would you do?" Well, first, it is rare when money is no object. But the idea is to do what the Epson brand proclaims. Exceed your vision.

I know a church that invested heavily in media facilities and infrastructure several years before the pandemic forced everyone online. When the church doors were shut, the media door swung widely open. Now, hundreds of thousands watch the Sunday live streams of the worship services. By God's direction, they exceeded their own vision.

Is there something beyond your vision right now? Is the Lord leading you to take steps in ministry or in life that don't make sense if we are only seeing through today's eyes? Abram, in the Old Testament, experienced this. God said "go," not saying where. And Abram went, taking his whole family to a foreign land. He trusted that the Lord who spoke to him had something in the future that exceeded Abram's vision in that day.

Author and inspirational speaker Simon Sinek says, "Great leaders must have two things: a vision of the world that does not yet exist and the ability to communicate that vision clearly."

We live in a communication age. If God has placed us in areas of leadership, we need to be able to bring others along toward that vision, even when they cannot see it clearly. As Christian leaders, we have the added responsibility to move others to God's agenda, the ultimate vision for all of us.

Drs. Henry and Richard Blackaby wrote a book on spiritual leadership. In it, they write about how important it is for a leader to know where the Lord is leading.

> It's surprising how many leaders settle for managing the day-to-day operations of their organization with no com-

prehensible idea of where God is leading them. Every decision is a step toward a destination.

SPIRITUAL LEADERSHIP, HENRY AND RICHARD BLACKABY

So, what is the destination the Lord has before you? What lies over the horizon for you, your family, and the organization or group you may lead? Are you willing to obey God's direction toward something you cannot see yet? Are you willing to be obedient to His call in your life as a leader?

Exceed your vision...and move others toward what the Spirit of the Lord is leading you to do in ministry.

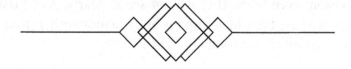

DAY SEVENTEEN

What are you willing to do?

Leaders often look back on their lives and work and review the path they have climbed to get to where they are today. And in looking back, they quietly say to themselves, "I'm glad I don't have to do all that again."

They would never say it out loud, but their heart is saying, "I'm above all that, now that I am a leader and in charge."

When I was a media minister, I had a seminary student intern who wanted to lead a church media ministry. One day, I asked him to coil up the big, long camera cables we had in our small studio. He looked at me and, either in words or facial expression, communicated, "It is beneath me to do that." The young man was about to learn a lesson from me.

In the years of our MEDIA Alliance ministry, I have licked envelopes, folded programs, set up tables and chairs at conferences, and performed many other menial tasks. To be honest, I didn't really think about it as being above me or below me. The task just needed to be done.

The founder of Bell Aircraft, Lawrence D. Bell, is quoted as saying, "Show me a man who cannot be bothered to do little things, and I'll show you a man who cannot be trusted to do big things."

Jesus was pretty clear about how we need to serve and where our hearts should be. He taught that the first should be last, and He demonstrated this as He washed the disciples' feet. Some of those chosen men struggled in that area. James and John, the sons of Zebedee, wanted something from Jesus.

> *"Arrange it," they said, "so that we will be awarded the highest places of honor in your glory—one of us at your right, the other at your left."*
>
> *Jesus said, "You have no idea what you're asking..."*
>
> MARK 10:37-38 MSG

I know that in leadership we need to delegate tasks to others, protect our time, and do the things that only we can do. But we also need to check ourselves to see where our heart is. Pride is a sneaky thing that can destroy a good and powerful ministry. Leadership expert John Maxwell is strong on leaders serving others in our ministries or organizations:

> I believe the bottom line in leadership isn't how far we advance ourselves but how far we advance others. That is achieved by serving others and adding value to their lives. I believe that God desires us not only to treat people with respect but also to actively reach out to them and serve them.
>
> THE 21 IRREFUTABLE LAWS OF LEADERSHIP

A word of warning: Don't do those menial tasks for show or announce to others what a great servant you are. Or pride will be knocking at your door.

Serve the Lord and others with gladness, and let the Lord lift you up.

DAY EIGHTEEN

Things not worth doing...

I love the humorous quote from Ken Blanchard.

> Things not worth doing are not worth doing well.

Have you ever come to the end of the day and wondered what you have accomplished? I have. Oh, sure, I filled my day with "stuff." But what did all that stuff amount to? Sometimes, we obsess about getting something done *well* that didn't need to be done at all. Or it could have been done by someone else (probably better).

Blanchard says, "Today people are often busy doing what seems to be extremely urgent but really isn't. They spend a great deal of time moving paper rather than listening to their people...." (Ken Blanchard, The Heart of a Leader)

Those last four words are key. Listening to their people. So often we are so focused on accomplishing a goal that we use our people instead of loving them and letting them feel good about accomplishing the goal. We dictate jobs and set timetables.

So how does a leader actually lead? One important ministry truth is that people need to like the leader they serve. Then they will follow, not out of duty or compliance or a paycheck, but out of a sense of mission set by a someone they admire. John Maxwell talks about the charisma that a leader needs.

> "THE GREATEST LEADERS HAVE IT—that special quality that causes people to be drawn to their magnetic personalities.... We all have the potential to develop this quality that makes the difference between personality and personality plus."
>
> BE A PEOPLE PERSON: EFFECTIVE LEADERSHIP
> THROUGH EFFECTIVE RELATIONSHIPS

This doesn't mean that you have to become something you aren't. It means you may need to develop some of the areas of your personality that help draw people to you and cause them to want to follow you. Nothing fake here...genuine care and concern for others.

Maxwell goes on to offer this acrostic for the word charisma.

- *Concern*
- *Help*
- *Action*
- *Results*
- *Influence*
- *Sensitivity*
- *Motivation*
- *Affirmation*

Without going into great detail, these are areas that can be developed in you that will ultimately help your ministry and the people who serve with you. You might examine your personality and style of leadership, then take two to three areas where you could improve. Maybe areas like concern, or sensitivity, or affirmation. What would it mean to your staff if you took the time to learn what things outside of work concerned them most? A brief time of prayer with this person on these things would be a great step toward building a better and more productive relationship. A word of caution. Don't do this with a sense of manipulation. There has to be real concern for the person and not just what they can do for the ministry. Jesus modeled this in the love and concern he showed for friends like Mary, Martha, and Lazarus. He wept real tears and experienced fellowship and joy with them, too. Then there is John, often referred to as the apostle that Jesus loved. So much so that from the cross, Jesus gave the assignment to John to care for His mother, Mary, which John faithfully did.

Paul gave his Roman friends this advice:

Don't think you are better than you really are. Be honest in your evaluation of yourselves, measuring yourselves by the faith God has given us.

Romans 12:3 NLT

Eugene Peterson expands on that and the surrounding verse with this:

I'm speaking to you out of deep gratitude for all that God has given me, and especially as I have responsibilities in relation to you. Living then, as every one of you does, in pure grace, it's important that you not misinterpret yourselves as people who are bringing this goodness to God. No, God brings it all to you. The only accurate way to understand ourselves is by what God is and by what he does for us, not by what we are and what we do for him.

If you are at the start of your day as you read this, think of the most important thing you can do today that will show your care and concern for those the Lord has entrusted to you as co-laborers in His work. You may need to go over that To-do list and mark out things you probably shouldn't be spending your valuable time on anyway.

If you are nearing the end of a busy day, ask yourself, "Did I do the most important things today, or just check off the urgent items?"

Then, vow to think of others first. Remember, there is no virtue in doing well something you shouldn't be doing at all.

DAY NINETEEN

Were the good old days really good?

Some friends at a broadcast ministry where I served years ago were texting about the adventures and memories of those times. And the phrase came up. Those were the "good old days." I had to answer them. "No...those weren't the good old days.

They were the GREAT old days.

That got me thinking about those days. Did we have challenges and problems? Absolutely. Did we have times when we didn't have the funds we needed to keep the ministry going and growing? Absolutely. So why did we think those days were great...or even good?

I believe it was in the struggle of those days that our outstanding team of servants pulled together even more than usual. Financial struggles caused us to tighten the ministry belt. I remember one staffer going around making sure the lights in the bathroom were turned off. Most folks used both sides of the yellow post-it notes. The monthly staff lunch became a time when each person brought their favorite food rather than the ministry ordering something, and we all shared. And we prayed through the difficult days for the Lord to bless.

The struggles of those days led to a stronger relationship among the staff and a real sense of joy as we overcame challenge after challenge. We prayed through the difficult days for the Lord to bless us, and He did. Despite the struggles, those times weren't just good days—they were great days.

Legendary American football coach Lou Holtz explains the importance of struggles in life this way:

> *"Show me someone who has done something worthwhile, and I'll show you someone who has overcome adversity."*

Blind Helen Keller reminds us to focus beyond today's downturns to what tomorrow may bring.

> "Be of good cheer. Do not think of today's failures, but of

the success that may come tomorrow. You have set yourself a difficult task, but you will succeed if you persevere, and you will find a joy in overcoming obstacles."

A joy in overcoming! That's a great perspective. And it is a good reminder that today's struggles and adversities are not the ultimate defining characteristics for us. How we handle the challenges is what makes the difference.

Solomon talked about what we learn from adversity.

If you fail under pressure, your strength is too small.

PROVERBS 24:10 NLT

Peter wrote about the rewards...the hope we have as we deal with life's challenges. See how Eugene Peterson paraphrased Peter's encouragement.

You're not the only ones plunged into these hard times. It's the same with Christians all over the world. So keep a firm grip on the faith. The suffering won't last forever. It won't be long before this generous God who has great plans for us in Christ—eternal and glorious plans they are!—will have you put together and on your feet for good. He gets the last word; yes, he does.

1 Peter 5:10-11 MSG

We face many challenges and adversities today. How will we see these days in ten or twenty years? We can look back and remember the struggles, defeats, and failures. Or we can see God's hand and respond with a positive attitude because of His promises. Then, we will see days that weren't just good—they were great! The Lord gave Joshua advice that serves us well today.

This is my command—be strong and courageous! Do not be afraid or discouraged. For the Lord your God is with you wherever you go.

Joshua 1:9 NLT

These challenging days can be tomorrow's "great old days" if you live in the light of God's promises.

DAY TWENTY

Distractions...I've had a few...

Singer Frank Sinatra felt that way about "regrets" as he crooned the song "My Way." Most of us today would feel that regrets have been eclipsed by distractions. The coronavirus of past years has been a global distraction, as well as a major health and economic concern. Racial unrest, political tensions, and protesters of all kinds draw our attention more than other things. Distractions. Sometimes, it is even the daily impact of our lives and deep needs in our service to the Lord. Distractions.

You may be asking, "Distractions from what?" Glad you asked.

The other morning, Judy and I were reading one of the accounts of Jesus feeding the enormous crowds that sometimes packed around Him to hear His teaching. In this account, Jesus gave a brief and stark response to His disciples when they talked to him about the crowd's hunger.

Late in the afternoon his disciples came to him and said, "This is a remote place, and it's already getting late. Send the crowds away so they can go to the nearby farms and villages and buy something to eat."

Mark 6:35-36 NLT

That sounds like a reasonable suggestion, right? Except for one thing. The disciples were distracted—distracted by the need, distracted by the lack of food for the masses, distracted by their meager resources. And in verse 37, what was Jesus' stark response?

"...You feed them."

Can you put yourself in the place of the disciples? They look out over the hillside at the five thousand men, along with women and children. Probably ten to fifteen thousand hungry folks. And then the disciples did what I probably would have done: weigh the options and the obstacles, try to strategize a way to do what the Master said, and come up short. Jesus' command to His disciples, "You feed them." The disciples' response?

> *"With what?" they asked. "We'd have to work for months to earn enough money to buy food for all these people!"*
>
> MARK 6:37 NLT

You can almost hear the frustration in their voices. Impossible task. Lacking resources. Yet a clear command from Jesus. I'm thinking there were several awkward seconds that passed as Jesus looked at his key leaders and they looked at Him.

We need to remember that these disciples had seen amazing things happen as Jesus ministered. Their Master had healed the sick, rescued people from demons, calmed the seas...miracle after miracle. But a lack of bread and a large crowd had somehow distracted them from the Lord's amazing power.

Are you making the application? God has called you to serve. You have great opportunities. You see the hand of the Lord at work in amazing ways. Then...some obstacle comes up. The need is too great. The resources are too little. The budget is too small. The donations are too few. On and on...distracted by the things we see. And we hear Jesus say, "YOU feed them. YOU do it."

How?

Jesus' plan was simple. What do you have? Bring it to me.

> *"How much bread do you have?" he asked. "Go and find out." They came back and reported, "We have five loaves of bread and two fish."*
>
> MARK 6:38 NLT

Yes, there are many challenges before us. Yes, the world is in turmoil. The global economy is teetering. There are the proverbial wars and rumors of wars. We have all sorts of obstacles. But Jesus' direction to the distracted disciples is just as true for us today. What DO you have? Bring it to me.

The few brief words in the opening verses of Hebrews 12 are the key.

> *"...keeping our eyes on Jesus...."*

You know the rest of the story. The people were fed from those meager resources. And as He does again and again, Jesus showed

His exceedingly abundant power and love as the disciples brought back more food than they started with. God will make a way...

Distracted? Keep your eyes on Jesus!

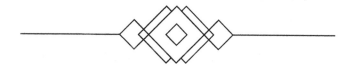

DAY TWENTY-ONE

A string and two cans...

Did you ever try the old string and can form of communication? As a kid (it was probably my Cub Scout days) I punched small holes in two cans (green beans, I think...though it doesn't matter). Then I threaded a string from the outside bottom of the can through the small hole and tied a knot large enough not to slip back through the hole. I repeated it with the other can. Then, with a buddy, we stretched the cans a distance away. One would speak into their can, and the other would listen. Then, we would reverse the roles. OK, it wasn't hi-fi or anything, but I could hear him, and he could hear me.

Communication. It was crude, but it worked. Do you know what the key element was in that process? That person on the other end of the can-string gizmo. Without my buddy, there would be no communication.

That truth, illustrated crudely in my Cub Scout days, stretches from the days of the Greek philosopher Aristotle to today. While his teacher and colleague Plato dealt more with content, Aristotle developed a theory of communication that takes into account more than the speaker and the content. Aristotle included the listener...the audience...in his equation and the outcome of the communication. Aristotle's five points in his theory of communication were these.

- Speaker
- Speech
- Occasion
- Audience
- Effect

This theory should still guide us in the communication process. It flows from the principle that we need to know our audience and what we want the communication to accomplish.

I love the Apostle Paul's speech to the Areopagites in Athens when he was invited to talk about this new "religion." Paul seized the occasion, understood his audience, and had firmly in mind the goal of his speech to these men. It is found in Acts 17.

"Men of Athens, I notice that you are very religious in every way, for as I was walking along I saw your many shrines. And one of your altars had this inscription on it: 'To an Unknown God.' This God, whom you worship without knowing, is the one I'm telling you about...."

Acts 17:22-23 NLT

Paul had done his homework. Having traveled to the great city of Athens, he had been distressed by all the statues and the Athenians' allegiance to all sorts of gods. He used that as an introduction to his speech. He even later quoted a Greek poet to help build a relationship with his audience. But his focus and purpose were always to preach Christ. He cleverly told them the "unknown god" they had built a statue to was the very one Paul wanted to share with them: Jesus.

Paul's homework was done to keep his audience listening. Without an audience, there would be no communication. I have stood on Mars Hill, looking down into the Agora and across to the Acropolis. I could have stood on the very spot where Paul spoke and given my finest speech. But unless there was an audience—another person on the other end of the string—there would be no real or effective communication.

If you broadcast, podcast, or just speak today, do you know who your audience is? Do you know if they are really tuned into you as you speak? Have you done your homework? Do you say things that relate to their world to help keep them tuned in and catch your message? If not...you may find there is no one on the other end of the string and tin can...and real communication is not happening.

Jesus was a master speaker. Ken Gosnell leads Christian CEOs and, in an article on Jesus and His example of communication, said, "Jesus always knew His audience. He spoke the right words to the right people with the right tone to deliver the right message."

So...is anyone on the other end of the string? Do you know who they are? Do you know how to draw them in? Do you have a plan and a purpose for your time speaking to them? Is communication really happening, or are you just speaking into the air? How critical is this communication process? Paul summed it up this way:

But how can they call on him to save them unless they believe in him? And how can they believe in him if they have never heard about him? And how can they hear about him unless someone tells them?

Romans 10:14 NLT

You have the tools. You have the plan. You have the message. Communicate God's Truth with your "audience" today.

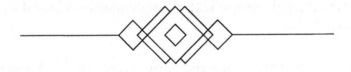

DAY TWENTY-TWO
What lasts?

We live in a throw-away world. There was a time when a fine Swiss watch was to be treasured. If it didn't keep accurate time or was broken, off it went to the watch repair shop. Then Timex came along. These watches were certainly not of the caliber of an Omega or TAG Heuer watch. They were inexpensive, reasonably accurate, and somewhat reliable. And if they broke...you tossed them and bought another. Increasingly that philosophy has carried through to other items we use in our world. Few people take the time or the trouble to fix something these days. Toss it and replace it.

Yet there are some things worth "repairing" versus replacing. We had a giclée print of a painting by a friend who has been the Artist Laureate of Texas. It became faded due to the sun shining into the room and on the wall where the painting hung. There was value to us because the painting reproduction was an artist's proof and was given to us by the artist himself. Thankfully, a cousin, who also is an artist, agreed to restore the original work by painting over it, matching the original colors and strokes. Her beautiful restoration work now hangs over the mantle on our fireplace. That artwork is now a twice-treasured item.

A while back, I attended memorial services for dear friends. Both individuals were outstanding in their crafts. Though they worked in different fields with different skills, people recognized them for their unusual ability to do things with a skill above anyone else. One was known as a master "fix-it" guy!

But that wasn't what impacted me.

As I listened to people, friends, family, step to the podium at these two services, what struck me was the lasting impact of the love these men exhibited through the time they gave to others. They willingly shared their skills and their expertise, yes. But it was the time and attention given freely to others that stood out. To these friends and family, this translated into the most lasting attribute of the lives these were remembering and honoring—love.

It is interesting that when Jesus was quizzed about the most important truths for a follower of Christ, it came down to this:

> *The most important commandment is this: '...The Lord our God is the one and only Lord. And you must love the Lord your God with all your heart, all your soul, all your mind, and all your strength.' The second is equally important: 'Love your neighbor as yourself.'*
>
> MARK 12:29-31 NLT

I have adapted and adopted that passage as my philosophy of life, and I seek to live that out in all I do.

Love God. Love people.

That is the overarching philosophy I aspire to in leadership: love—for God, and because of that love, I have a love for those God sends my way. Four words, profound impact.

Love God. Love people.

Do you take time to listen to others, even when you don't have time? Are you willing to share your expertise with others who might be a bit further back on the path, even when you are busy with something else? What about your family, the most important mission field the Lord has given you? Time? Attention? Do you freely give it?

When I sit through meaningful memorial services, my mind reflects on my dear friends and the time and love I received from them. It drives me to want to live that same way each day of my life. The Apostle Paul wrote to the Corinthians about the things that are most important—things that will last even beyond our years on earth. He concluded his brief treatise on the subject with these simple words.

> *Three things will last forever—faith, hope, and love—and the greatest of these is love.*
>
> 1 CORINTHIANS 13:13 NLT

Strive for what will last...not just for our days here, but for all eternity. Love.

DAY TWENTY-THREE
That's impossible!

It is amusing to see incidents in the Bible when God's people ask for a miracle, the Lord does that miraculous thing, and the people are shocked and surprised. It is amusing, that is, until I see it in my life and the life of other Christ-followers. Examples?

There is that miracle of Jesus feeding the five thousand men... plus women and children. When the disciples encouraged Jesus to send the people home because they had no food for them and no way to get any, Jesus simply looked at his dedicated followers and said, "You feed them." Surprise!

Later, when the disciples had pushed off from shore while Jesus stayed to pray, the storm hit, and it hit hard. Looking around, these men saw a form walking on the water. Jesus. And Peter, being Peter, blurted out a request.

Then Peter called to him, "Lord, if it's really you, tell me to come to you, walking on the water." "Yes, come," Jesus said.

MATTHEW 14:28,29 NLT

You remember what happened next. Peter jumped over the side of the boat, and he walked on water—until. Until he looked around at his circumstances—the winds and the big waves—and he began to sink. Peter had apparently never sung the song, "He who began a good work in you...." And Jesus, in His love and with His gentle admonition, grabbed Peter and exclaimed, "You have so little faith. Why did you doubt me?"

I've prayed for friends and family members for years and have seen the Lord do His miraculous things in their lives. Yes, some are still a work in progress—but aren't we all? There are times Jesus has had to say in my heart, "You have so little faith. Why did you doubt me?"

There have been other times when I have brought problems to the Lord, looking for Him to do something great before my eyes, and He has responded as He did to His disciples, "You feed them." As I imagine those men who surrounded Jesus did, I sometimes just stand before the Lord and stare. "What? I just told you the impossible situation we are in. Don't you get it, God?"

Oh, He gets it. And He understands you and me. The Lord knows we need to take steps of faith in our ministries, in our lives, and with our families. If Christ is leading us, then we need to just step out of the boat or begin to gather little fish and loaves of bread.

As you read God's Word, as you pray, as you help and lead others this week, listen for the Lord's voice in your heart.

"Trust Me."
"Keep your eyes on Me."
"Yes, step out of the boat."

And don't be surprised when the impossible becomes not only possible but amazingly victorious.

DAY TWENTY-FOUR

Turn on the power...

When I was a young boy, my dad owned a radio repair shop in downtown Fort Worth. I loved to rummage around in the old radios and see if I could get any of them working. I learned that there were some key vacuum tubes that were critical to making the radio power up and provide music, news, information, and even inspiration to those who listened. One tube was a 6AU6. That tube allowed all of the other tubes to function and amplify the programming picked up by the radio. When that tube went bad, the radio was merely a useless box.

I learned recently that Jim Meyer, president of SiriusXM satellite radio, uses an interesting acrostic in his meetings. He references the acrostic over and over to his team. It is based on the word A-M-P-L-I-F-Y. Sounds like it fits right into our communication world. Here is his acrostic:

- Applaud and encourage new thinking.
- Move forward and be purposeful in our desire to win.

- Prioritize honesty, integrity, and respectful communication.
- Lean on each other and learn from one another.
- Invest in our actions and commit to the follow-through.
- Find ways to give back by focusing on community and feeding your individuality.
- You Matter.

Some good thoughts there. These principles promote fresh thinking with great purpose and desire. They seek to build a foundation of honesty, integrity, and respect with all in our communications. Teamwork, community, and the value of each person on the team are emphasized.

While certainly not a biblical approach, explaining the acrostic can have spiritual meaning as we lead others. Look at what God's Word says in some of these areas.

For I am about to do something new. See, I have already begun! Do you not see it? I will make a pathway through the wilderness. I will create rivers in the dry wasteland.

ISAIAH 43:19 NLT

...let us strip off every weight that slows us down, especially the sin that so easily trips us up. And let us run with endurance the race God has set before us.

HEBREWS 12:1 NLT

He grants a treasure of common sense to the honest. He is a shield to those who walk with integrity.

PROVERBS 2:7 NLT

Give your complete attention to these matters. Throw yourself into your tasks so that everyone will see your progress.

1 TIMOTHY 4:15 NLT

We who are strong must be considerate of those who are sensitive about things like this. We must not just please ourselves.

ROMANS 15:1 NLT

I'm sure you could find more from God's word that amplifies the acrostic A-M-P-L-I-F-Y. More importantly than just finding scripture or reciting an acrostic, put these principles to work as you serve the Lord for His glory and His purpose. And see God's power turned on and amplified through you.

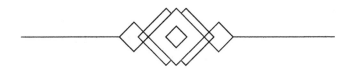

DAY TWENTY-FIVE
Don't out-think yourself...

Our world is complicated and complex. If we are not careful, we will overthink situations and solutions that we need for our ministries and organizations. Sometimes, simplicity is best. But in this complex world of technology, simplicity isn't usually our first thought. Maybe it ought to be.

Many of us have sung the simple chorus, "Oh, How He Loves You and Me," by the late Christian composer, pianist, and conductor Kurt Kaiser. I had the honor of getting to know Kurt over the years. On one occasion, I drove 90 miles south of my home to his home in Waco, Texas. We sat in his office/studio, and he told me how that simple song came about.

Kurt wanted a little chorus for a project he was working on. As happens with artists and creative people, his mind was blank. Nothing would come. Looking around in his piano bench, he came across a little piece of paper with some words on it he had written sometime before. Just a few words, discard when written but found in this moment of creative need.

Kurt set the piece of paper on the music rack of his piano and began to look for a melody that would fit those few simple words. What he arrived at was a sweet, simple chorus that resonated with people because of its simple truth.

> O how He loves you and me,
> O how He loves you and me.
> He gave His life, what more could He give?
> O how He loves you; O how He loves me;
> O how He loves you and me!

In Kurt's words:

> "In 1975, I sat down to think about that phrase and the whole song quickly came to me. I could not have spent more than 10 or 15 minutes writing the whole of it. That's how rapidly it all came, the lyrics and the melody together. I sent it off to secure a copyright. I could not believe what came back in the mail."

To his surprise, Kurt received a letter back from that office saying,

"Mr. Kaiser, thank you for submitting your song for copyright. I'm sorry to inform you there is not enough original material for us to be able to legally protect it with a copyright." The song was simply too simple.

Kurt, being the creative man that he was, quickly penned a second verse to the chorus, never intending it to be sung, only to secure that important copyright.

> Jesus to Calv'ry did go,
> His love for sinners to show.
> What He did there brought hope from despair.
> O how He loves you; O how He loves me;
> O how He loves you and me!

That day, Kurt Kaiser played that simple song for me in his studio/office. Even as I write these words, I tear up at the simple truth—the profound truth—of God's amazing love for me and for you. It is powerful.

Interestingly, during that visit, Kurt put on a tape of that song. Kurt Kaiser was a great improviser, and he took the simple melody of that simple song and woven it into an almost 10-

minute piano piece as intricate as a classical piece by Debussy. The simple had taken on new life.

A few years later the Christian station I served had a special concert with a large symphony orchestra. Kurt was in the audience, and we had arranged a surprise. We called him up on stage at the symphony hall. He sat down at the grand piano, and before thousands in that great concert hall, Kurt played that extended version of his simple chorus. Several times in the piece, he would nod to the audience, and they would begin to voice those simple words, softly...reverently...thoughtfully.

> O how He loves you and me,
> O how He loves you and me.
> He gave His life, what more could He give?
> O how He loves you; O how He loves me;
> O how He loves you and me!

I will never forget that moment. The simple had become profound. Tears fell from many eyes. Professional musicians sat up in surprise. God was honored, and His Truth was lifted in praise.

Sometimes—sometimes—the simple idea is the right idea. And as a gentle reminder, it is not our idea that is important, simple or complex. It is the power of the Lord Jesus that is crucial.

He gave His life...what more could he give?

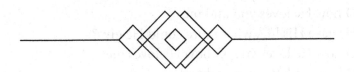

DAY TWENTY-SIX
The Medium is the Message

This intriguing phrase, "the medium is the message," has been shaping media thought for over 50 years, penned by Canadian communication thinker Marshall McLuhan in 1964. And it has probably confused as many people as it enlightened. In its simplest form, the thought is an acknowledgment that messages are not delivered in a vacuum but rather are impacted by the medium by which they are carried. McLuhan goes a lot farther than that, but it is good to think through this concept as we transmit God's message.

On a greater level, those who are called to lead others, whether in our ministries, organizations, churches, or simply our families, need to understand a similar principle.

The character of a leader counts.

I know, we see many leaders whose personal character is questionable. If they are leading well, it is only by God's abundant grace. But rather than consider these anomalies in leadership, let's think about the role to which God has called us.

In the book *Spiritual Leadership Coaching*, authors Richard Blackaby and Bob Royall talk about the importance of character for those wanting to lead others and connect them to God's plan and His heart. Dr. Blackaby talks about the difficulty of actually influencing others in a positive way.

> "Most people want to impact others, yet such influence is often elusive.... The sheer number or volume of a person's words does not determine their power. Even truthful words may fail to inspire change. The most effective coaches are those whose character is consistent with their message."

That sounds a lot like Marshall McLuhan's thoughts. The medium, the person wanting to lead others, influences greatly the message. Our ability to lead others spiritually is often limited by our own spiritual condition. Dr. Henry Blackaby said, "You cannot take people further spiritually than you have gone yourself."

So, if you want to give strong, spiritual leadership to those the Lord has entrusted to you—your staff, volunteers, family, friends—there are some things to keep in mind. We know that if we want radio listeners to hear specific programming and receive the message we have for them, they must be sure they are tuned in to the correct radio frequency. In the book on spiritual leadership, the authors point out that coaches and leaders must be tuned in to God's frequency in order to hear God's message and direction. And there are four ways that happens.

- God speaks through the Bible. Coaches and leaders must persistently seek the Person and will of God through His Word.

- God speaks through prayer. However, simply telling God about a need does not necessarily reveal God's answers. For that, people must stop speaking and tune their spiritual senses to the Lord's voice.

- God sometimes speaks through life circumstances. Blackaby calls this "connecting the spiritual dots." We must learn to recognize the Lord's activity in our ordinary lives. Life is merely a random series of events...until people recognize God's activity in their circumstances.

- God speaks through the church. Spiritual communities provide valuable wisdom, feedback, and accountability to their participants.

Author Greg Henry Quinn's thoughts on character ring true:

> "Some are blessed with physical and mental facility, but none are more prized than the one who has developed true character."

Famed American basketball coach John Wooden would agree. "Ability may get you to the top, but it takes character to keep you there."

Paul, writing to the Roman believers, talked about the steps that lead to a person of character.

> *Not only this, but we also rejoice in sufferings, knowing that suffering produces endurance, and endurance, character, and character, hope.*
>
> ROMANS 5:3-4 NET

To sum up the importance of character, here's what Blackaby and Royall say:

> "The key to a coach's (or leader's) effectiveness is not in their eloquence but their Christ-likeness."

That is my prayer for you and for me today.

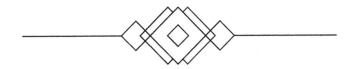

DAY TWENTY-SEVEN

Success! Now what?

I was intrigued recently by John Maxwell's comments in the Maxwell Leadership Bible. He looked at Nehemiah's response and action after the successful rebuilding of the wall around Jerusalem, and from this biblical passage in the Old Testament, Maxwell drew some interesting leadership insight.

Many of us set goals and have projects for our ministries and organizations that stretch us and often exhaust us. If we are not careful, we can let down our guard, enjoy the success of the project or event, and fail to lead properly. What was it that Nehemiah did that Maxwell caught? Nehemiah didn't let down his guard. If you read the beginning of Nehemiah 7 you see that the massive work of rebuilding the wall and hanging the gates had been finished in spite of opposition and ridicule. It would have been easy to celebrate and relax. Not Nehemiah.

This amazing man of God quickly gave specific instructions about watching and guarding the gate to the city of Jerusalem.

He recognized the importance of taking the next step in being not just successful but diligent and obedient to the Lord.

John Maxwell says that leaders must be willing to change their leadership style and stay on task even after a successful project or event.

> "Two emotions usually follow a great achievement: first, a sigh of relief and celebration; and second, a sense of . . . now what? How we handle achievement tells us a lot about our character."

Maxwell sees Nehemiah as a great example of how a leader needs to change with the times.

If a leader, especially after a great success or achievement, doesn't move from one season to the next, the ministry may suffer. Nehemiah knew they couldn't just celebrate the achievement of rebuilding the wall and gates. They needed to be diligent and have a plan for protecting the city and the people. He kept the success going by following up, organizing, and putting other people in his plan.

You may not feel you have an enemy ready to storm the gates, but we know that Satan is always roaming, looking for a weak place in our lives and our ministries to exploit and defeat us. Be sure that you, as a spiritual leader, adjust your plans and your style to ensure Satan doesn't get a foothold for destruction.

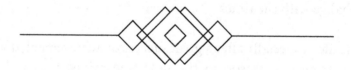

DAY TWENTY-EIGHT

The world's best tutor...

When I was in school, tutors weren't so prevalent. You didn't hear terms like "mentor" or "life coach" much back then. I know I could have used tutors for some of the classes I took in grade school and my undergraduate years. But now we have a wealth of help for those who are still on the education track. And since I am a proponent of being a lifelong learner, I'm glad there is help along that path, too.

It has been my privilege to sit under the teaching of great pastors and Bible scholars. I did not have formal seminary training, so I'm really glad for the wisdom of those who did and who have poured God's wisdom into me through all my years. I recognize the importance of studying God's Word myself, but I sometimes struggle with what it might mean and what the Lord is trying to tell me and teach me. Anyone one else find themselves there? I know how important it is to share more than good ideas... to share God's ideas.

In my Scripture reading recently, I came across the very familiar story of Jesus on the road to Emmaus. I love that passage. Do you remember? After Jesus' crucifixion, burial, and resurrection, one of the first places He was seen was on a dusty road out of Jerusalem. A couple of the Christ-followers were walking rather dejectedly away from their disappointment and despair over what had transpired. It was the worst of all days for them. Then Jesus began to walk alongside them.

After Jesus led them through the Scriptures and later revealed Himself to them, the men exclaimed...

> *Didn't our hearts burn within us as he talked with us on the road and explained the Scriptures to us?*
>
> *Luke 24:32 NLT*

That verse has touched me each time I have read it. But this time, something different emerged. It was the fact that Jesus explained the Scriptures to them. Jesus. One of the first things He did after the significant event of His resurrection was to walk among disciples and show them what the Word of God meant. And it changed the story for these men immediately.

If Jesus is the same yesterday, today, and forever—and He is—couldn't I expect that His Spirit would be willing to explain Scripture to me? Yes, there is value in commentaries, pastors, and teachers. But we should not think that we cannot discern God's Truth with His help on a daily basis.

It helps me in this area to ask some questions.

1. What is the passage saying? Context is critical.
2. What is the implication for the people of that day? How did they respond?
3. What is God saying to me? What does this mean for me personally...today?

In his book *Man: The Dwelling Place of God*, A. W. Tozer addressed the idea that the Bible is difficult to understand.

> "I believe that we find the Bible difficult because we try to read it as we would read any other book, and it is not the same as any other book.... The Bible is a supernatural book and can be understood only by supernatural aid."

How important is it to read and discern God's will in His Word? Dr. Henry Blackaby, in Experiencing God, reveals the value of dedicated, consistent spiritual growth.

> "Grass that is here today and gone tomorrow does not require much time to mature. A giant oak tree that lasts for generations requires much more time to grow strong."

Do you desire to understand God's Word and His will in your life on a daily basis? The good news is that you have the best tutor ever to help you interpret Scripture and apply it to your life...so that you might grow into the spiritual oak tree that God wants you to be.

DAY TWENTY-NINE

Check your ego...

How's your ego? One of the most challenging things for those who lead is dealing with ego—with pride. If things go well, we tend to pat ourselves on the back for the good planning and the good leadership we give, which results in success. If things go wrong, we can come up with a whole list of reasons why our plan failed. Others didn't execute our good plan as well as they should have. Situational timing caused the plan to miss the mark. Our ego works to keep us on top and others below us.

Someone has said, "A bad day for your ego is a great day for your soul." That may be a good starting point for us today. Taming our ego—our pride—is one of the most challenging things for us and one of the key areas where Satan does his work. Sadly, most of us don't realize the amazing potential that awaits us if we can just let go of our pride, control our ego, and embrace God's plan. The Lord speaks directly about this issue. James said it well.

> *Humble yourselves before the Lord, and he will lift you up in honor.*
>
> JAMES 4:10 NLT

I like what Ken Blanchard says about EGO. In his book *Lead Like Jesus*, Blanchard equates our human ego to an acronym. EGO equals Edging God Out. That really says it, doesn't it? When our ego takes over, we claim praise for ourselves that rightly should go to God. We tend to forget that anything we have, think, or do...anything...is a result of God's grace in our lives. The Lord gives us breath. He brings about circumstances and experiences that help us develop and grow as leaders. And His Spirit provides inspiration to our thoughts. Yet we often simply Edge God Out and let our ego take over. We claim praise that belongs to the Lord and take it as our own. Edging God Out. And that is dangerous.

Through Jeremiah the prophet, the Lord admonishes us.

> *This is what the Lord says:*
> *"Don't let the wise boast in their wisdom,*
> *or the powerful boast in their power,*
> *or the rich boast in their riches.*

*But those who wish to boast
should boast in this alone:
that they truly know me and understand that I am the
Lord who demonstrates unfailing love
and who brings justice and righteousness to the earth,
and that I delight in these things.*

I, the Lord, have spoken!

JEREMIAH 9: 23-24 NLT

Ken Blanchard offers another acronym for EGO that we would be wise to embrace.

EGO=Exalt God Only.

That means doing what Jeremiah wrote those thousands of years ago...boast only that we know God and understand and acknowledge that He alone is God...and we aren't!

One of the warning signs that we are Edging God Out, according to Blanchard, is the constant use of the pronoun "I". I did this. I deserve that. My plans, my ideas—And on and on. Take inventory of your own language and see how many times you fall into this trap. A phrase like, "If the Lord allows..." should be more than a trite slogan. It should permeate all we do. And we need to quickly and sincerely add at the end of an accomplishment, "Praise God for His great work in my life."

Solomon, the wisest man who ever lived, gave good advice.

> *Pride leads to disgrace,*
> *but with humility comes wisdom.*
>
> PROVERBS 11:2 NLT

So...what will it be for you and your ego. Will you Edge God Out? Or will you, more and more, day by day, Exalt God Only? The decision is yours. The glory belongs to the Lord.

DAY THIRTY

Cynicism? Yeah...sure!

I was about to interview my friend Chuck Swindoll at a listener event several years ago. Dr. Swindoll has been one of the top biblical teachers in the U. S. and has been featured on the radio program Insight for Living since its start in 1979. That program airs weekly on over two thousand radio stations worldwide. At our listener event, there were almost two thousand people, and as I started my first questions to Chuck, he interrupted me...and startled me.

"Ron, how do you keep from becoming cynical?" Chuck asked. That "out of the blue," left-field question left me speechless—for a moment. To be honest, I'm not exactly sure how I responded. I probably talked about keeping the focus on Jesus and on our calling to serve Him. For whatever reason, cynicism was on Chuck Swindoll's mind that day.

Mentor and leadership coach Fred Smith also has thoughts about cynicism:

> "Cynicism has no integrity. Even though it often properly evaluates the present, it has no hope for the future."

The Israelites lacked hope for the future even though they witnessed the amazing power of God to save them from Egyptian slavery. Yet their cynical nature came out verbally again and again. Listen to their comments to Moses, their leader:

> *"Why did you bring us out here to die in the wilderness? Weren't there enough graves for us in Egypt? What have you done to us? Why did you make us leave Egypt? Didn't we tell you this would happen while we were still in Egypt? We said, 'Leave us alone! Let us be slaves to the Egyptians. It's better to be a slave in Egypt than a corpse in the wilderness!'"*
>
> EXODUS 14:11-12 NLT

That's being pretty cynical!

Jonathan Parnell, a pastor in Minneapolis, Minnesota, has some frank words about this kind of attitude that can sneak into our lives:

"Cynicism is that sneering bitterness toward all things true and deep. It's the subtle contempt trying to contaminate the cheeriest of moments — that slow, thick smoke of pessimism toxifying the oxygen in the lungs of our hope...."

That's a good warning for us to be on guard.

The apostle Peter, in his letter to new believers, may have been addressing this skeptical attitude as people looked for the promises of the Lord to unfold:

> *The Lord isn't really being slow about his promise, as some people think. No, he is being patient for your sake. He does not want anyone to be destroyed, but wants everyone to repent.*
>
> 2 PETER 3:9 NLT

Fred Smith concluded with these thoughts:

"As Christians we have the responsibility to accurately assess the environment and respond appropriately. Maturity allows us to see without falling into unhealthy cynicism. We always want to be realistic but keep our minds centered on the truth of the higher things."

I like that. Be centered on the truth of the higher things. Let's fix our hearts and minds on the higher things and cast aside any cynical or pessimistic attitude that may be starting to creep in.

As Paul said:

> *"Fix your thoughts on what is true, and honorable, and right, and pure, and lovely, and admirable. Think about things that are excellent and worthy of praise."*
>
> PHILIPPIANS 4:8 NLT

God is worthy of our praise.

DAY THIRTY-ONE

Too good to be true?

You've heard that phrase, "If it seems too good to be true, it probably is." That used to be reserved for people making financial investments in schemes or projects. But in these days of internet and social media, we can all fall into that trap.

Full disclosure. I've done it myself. I would see a "special deal" and feel I just couldn't pass up such a bargain. The stark reality hits later. I should have checked further. Thankfully, the impact was relatively minor.

Part of a passage from an Old Testament story deals with a much bigger impact. Right after Joshua and the Israelites entered the Promised Land, they went into battle. Jericho turned out to be a victory as the people followed God's commands. Watching those walls fall should have taught God's people something.

But right on the heels of that victory, they were defeated by a small army from Ai. There was sin in the Israelite camp. Achan had not heeded the Lord's direction, and the result was defeat.

After God dealt with Achan and his family, Israel defeated the army of Ai. Lesson learned? Follow God's directions? Not exactly. Soon, some travelers showed up in worn clothes with old-looking wineskins, moldy bread, and worn-out sandals. They said they were from a distant land, and the Israelite leaders bought their lie. And here is the verse that caught my attention:

> *So the Israelites examined their food, but they did not consult the Lord.*
>
> JOSHUA 9:14 NLT

They did not consult the Lord.

How many times have we ventured out in ministry and life and failed to consult the Lord? How much time, energy, and resources have we invested in a project that we thought was good, yet we failed to consult the Lord?

Not everything that sounds good IS good. Not every idea is a good idea. Not every strategy is a godly strategy. How do we discern the good idea from the godly idea?

They failed to consult the Lord.

That phrase resonates in my mind and heart. James said we often don't have what the Lord intended for us for a simple reason.

...you don't have what you want because you don't ask God for it.

JAMES 4:2 NLT

James goes on to point out that we fail by not asking with the right motives.

Direction for growth. Challenges facing the ministry. Issues with people. Family relationships. All of these require us to seek the Lord and His ways...and His timing.

Then, see what our God will do in and through us as we consult Him and follow His direction and plans for our lives and our ministries.

DAY THIRTY-TWO

Ready or not...

When I was a kid, we would gather all the other kids in the neighborhood and play outdoor games. One of my favorites was Hide and Seek. The name says it all. One person had to close their eyes while everyone else found a place to hide. Soon, the designated "seeker" would yell out, "Ready or not, here I come." Then, he or she would begin to look for the people who were hiding. Simpler days back then, for sure.

Sometimes, on our personal journeys, we want to yell out, "Wait, I'm not ready!" God puts a challenge before us, and we want to know more details before we are willing to commit. We aren't ready, and we aren't going.

Pastor and author Mark Batterson says that is bad thinking. Using the life of Abraham as an example, Batterson says we have it all wrong.

"You'll never be ready. You'll never be ready to get married.

> You'll never be ready to have kids. You'll never be ready to start a business or go back to school or move to the mission field.... You'll never have enough faith, enough cash, or enough courage."

Batterson goes on to say, "I never have been, and I'm sure I never will be, ready for anything God has called me to do."

The writer of Hebrews points out that how Abraham lived is how we should live our life of faith. When God called Abraham, "He went without knowing where he was going." (Hebrews 11:9 NLT) If that were us today, we would likely want a long-term plan before we stepped out in faith.

Does that mean we shouldn't plan or use our wisdom and experience in our long-term decision-making? Not at all. We don't need to take a thoughtless or prayerless approach on our spiritual journey. But it does mean that we need to be ready to move on whatever revelation the Lord shares with us.

Batterson says we need to adopt the attitude, "Why not?" Dare to dream. Dare to take God at His word without knowing the whole story. If you spend all your time getting ready, you may miss the wonderful adventure that the Lord has for you.

The best illustration in my personal life was the launching of our global ministry, MEDIA Alliance International. At a time when many of my friends were retiring, heading to the golf course, or hitting the road in an RV, I sensed God leading me to start this nonprofit ministry. It meant we would have to raise all the resources. We would have to start from scratch designing a ministry with worldwide impact. And we would do it with no staff. On paper (and in some people's minds), it didn't make sense. I guess in my heart, I was saying, "Why not." OK, there could have been many reasons why not. But I didn't let those things deter me from what I sensed the Lord wanted me to do. Gratefully, my wife Judy was in full agreement. And there were others who encouraged me as we took the first steps. Trusting in God's provision overrode the fear that could have stopped me.

Over ten years later, by God's direction, MEDIA Alliance works with dynamic ministry partners in over forty-five countries and has virtual offices in four key regions of the world. Fifteen thousand Christians in media ministries have been trained and encouraged as they serve, often in challenging places.

If we are not careful, we can become so afraid of doing the wrong thing that we keep from doing the right thing. Abraham didn't know where he was going or what would be there when he arrived, but his focus was on following the Lord. Abraham was obedient to the revelation God had given him, and the writer of Hebrews puts him in the Hall of Fame of the Lord's faithful servants.

What is God telling you? What does He want you to do? Ask yourself, "Why not?"

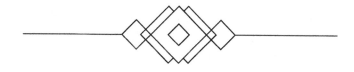

DAY THIRTY-THREE
Why settle for less?

I've heard that phrase in advertisements for decades. You probably have, too. The announcer extols the virtues of a product that is "superior to any other." And then he intones, "Why settle for less?"

What is amazing is how many times we do settle for less. Not just on consumer products but in how we live and how we serve the Lord. Less than the best.

Media producer, consultant, and author Phil Cooke recently wrote on our current culture and the things that keep us from holding up a high standard for ourselves, our ministry work, and those we lead. Among the things he listed were these:

<u>The Fear of Offending</u>

In a culture that values being politically correct and avoiding offense, there's a hesitancy to give critical feedback or point out flaws. Constructive criticism or holding individuals to high standards might be perceived as harsh or confrontational, leading to a reluctance to push for excellence.

Mediocrity in the Name of Kindness

The desire to be 'nice' often translates to accepting mediocrity rather than demanding excellence. Settling for average or 'good enough' becomes the norm to avoid potentially hurting someone's feelings or causing discomfort.

Embracing the Average

The fear of being labeled as 'mean' or 'unpleasant' often leads to a culture that rewards mediocrity. Embracing and celebrating average performance over striving for excellence sets a standard that's lower than what is truly achievable.

Then Phil nailed it when he said, "...when we stop inspiring excellence in our team, we're undermining everyone's potential."

Settling for less than the best has long-term consequences, not just a short-term deficit. If we don't hold ourselves to a high standard, we are limiting the potential of each member of our team.

This is even more critical when we apply this to the personal and spiritual. Do we settle for less in our relationship with the Lord? Do we offer less than our best in our service to Christ? Do we compare our offering—our lives, and our service—to what Christ did on the cross? God gave His very best, His son Jesus, so we might have fellowship with Him for all eternity. What is our commitment to Almighty God? Oswald Chambers called it "Our Utmost for His Highest."

Paul wrote to the believers at Ephesus, commending them for their faith and pointing out what God did for them and for us.

> *I pray that your hearts will be flooded with light so that you can understand the confident hope he has given to those he called—his holy people who are his rich and glorious inheritance. I also pray that you will understand the incredible greatness of God's power for us who believe him.*
>
> EPHESIANS 1:18-19 (NLT)

Let your heart be flooded with God's greatness poured out for you. And let your work be a reflection of the excellence the Lord has shown you, so others may understand God's great love. In Jesus' words from Matthew 5:16...

...let your good deeds shine out for all to see, so that everyone will praise your heavenly Father.

Let's give the Lord our best, and not settle for anything less.

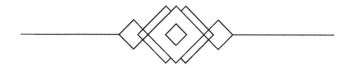

DAY THIRTY-FOUR

What are you known for?

What is your legacy? What do people say about you when your name is mentioned? What will be carved on your tombstone?

Fred Smith wanted his tombstone to say, "He Stretched Others." I like that.

What started me thinking about this topic was an obscure verse in the list of "begats" that often bog us down in our Bible reading and study.

I make it my routine to read through the Bible each year. And some passages are just like slogging through the mud. But when I stick to it, I'm often rewarded with a surprise, a nugget, a nudge from the Lord.

So, a few mornings ago, I was in Genesis 36 reading the long list of the descendants of the people, and I came across this:

> *The descendants of Zibeon were Aiah and Anah. (This is the Anah who discovered the hot springs in the wilderness while he was grazing his father's donkeys.)*
>
> Genesis 36:24 NLT

What is so special about that? Why was it even mentioned? Moses, the writer, wanted to be sure the reader knew which person he was talking about. So, he mentioned Anah was the one who found the hot springs in the wilderness. I can see the readers of that day saying, "Oh, THAT Anah!" And I also suspect they would be thinking of the blessing that hot spring was to them. And maybe there would be a bit of gratitude.

Most of the time, we don't think of our legacy. We may think of our children or grandchildren and the influence we might have on them. But I believe there is more to it than that. I believe God wants us to be a source of refreshment to those around us so that at some point down the road, people will hear your name and say, "That's the one who..."

As I have thought about that curious passage, I realized there is a lesson to be learned. Here is my take:

- Anah was doing what his father assigned him to do. He was willing to be obedient to his (earthly) father, and in doing that, he built a legacy.

- Anah was willing to do a menial, maybe even boring task, day after day after day. I have to believe that grazing donkeys wasn't a "plum job" for anyone. But he was willing.

- In performing a menial and low-level task, this man discovered something that blessed others. Others could partake of the soothing hot spring waters and be grateful.

How important was finding a hot spring in the wilderness? I don't know, except that God saw to it that, under the direction of the Holy Spirit, it was included in God's Holy Word for us to see and possibly learn from.

So...what will people say about you? About me? Are you willing to do what our Father "assigns" you to do, even if it is a rather menial task? If so, there could be a surprise discovery right around the corner.

DAY THIRTY-FIVE
Bible quiz time...

Who was Bartholomew (sometimes referred to as Nathanael)? If you said one of the twelve disciples, you get a gold star.

Now, what do you know about this man? That's where I got stuck the other morning. It dawned on me that I know almost nothing about this follower of Jesus except that the Lord called him to be one of those in His inner circle of twelve men. Scholars believe Bartholomew and Nathanael to be one and the same. If so, Bartholomew is the first recorded person to declare Jesus to be the "Son of God." And Jesus said of him, "He is a man in whom there is nothing false."

That's pretty much all we know. Yes, Bartholomew was among the twelve that Jesus sent out to perform miracles and to share Christ. Yes, he was with the others at the Lord's supper in the upper room. And he was among those who watched as Jesus ascended into heaven.

But there is nothing else about him in the Bible.

So, what is my point? Many followers of Christ receive no recognition. They get no "press." They serve faithfully and do so in obscurity. That goes against our culture today. We think we need to be honored and recognized to know if we are really effective in serving the Lord. Not so.

Oswald Chambers taught about this several times. In the book *So Send I You*, we read this:

> Jesus warned His disciples that they would be treated as nobodies; He never said they would be brilliant or marvelous. We all have a lurking desire to be exhibitions for God, to be put, as it were, in His showroom.

Adoniram Judson, an American missionary to Burma for forty years, once said:

> "Permit us to labor on in obscurity, and at the end of twenty years, you may hear from us again."

The Apostle Paul came at this subject another way:

> *Work willingly at whatever you do, as though you were working for the Lord rather than for people. Remember that the Lord will give you an inheritance as your reward, and that the Master you are serving is Christ.*
>
> COLOSSIANS 3:23-24 NLT

That verse may have led Oswald Chambers to ask:

> "If God chooses to have you labor in total obscurity, what is that to you?"

No, we may not make it into the world's "Hall of Fame." Yet we have the assurance that no matter how little people know of our efforts or even how much attention we may receive, we can all look forward to those words spoken by a master to His faithful follower:

> *"Well done, good and faithful servant."*

That should be enough.

DAY THIRTY-SIX

Light...or life?

There is an old hymn we used to sing:

> The whole world was lost in the darkness of sin.
> The Light of the world is Jesus.

I don't hear it much these days, but the message is as true today—maybe more so—than when I was young and singing those words.

As I travel to various places in our world, as I look across the spiritual landscape, it is quite obvious that our world is in darkness and needs a great light. The Light of the world.

Yet most in darkness don't see the Light. They often aren't aware they need the Light. Oh, yes, many know that something is not right in their world, or more specifically, in their lives. But they don't know what to do. Where to turn.

That's why Jesus, the Light of the world, said to His followers:

You are the light of the world....

MATTHEW 5:14 NLT

The Lord went on to say that our light should shine into the darkness in a way that points others to Him, that glorifies our Heavenly Father.

Henry Blackaby in his book *Experiencing God Day by Day* wrote:

> "There is no mistaking the effect of light upon a darkened place. Light boldly and unabashedly announces its presence and vigorously dispels darkness."

Can I expand that just a bit? It is one thing to carry the light, to shine the light, to hold up a spiritual mirror and reflect the light. It is another thing to live in the light. Today, I would say we need to hear, "Let your *life* so shine before men that they see Jesus and glorify our Heavenly Father." Yes, I can and should tell others what God's Word says. Far better if my life also shows others that we are living and walking in that light *personally*.

Blackaby went further in his writing:

> "God's desire is to fill you with His light. He wants you to shine as a brilliant testimony of His presence and power in your life, so that the darkness in the lives of those around you will be displaced by the light of God's glory. Can that be said of you as well? Do your coworkers recognize the light that is within you? Does the presence of Christ radiate from your home into your community? When God's light is allowed to shine unhindered through your life, the darkness around you will be dispelled."

There are many around you who need light. Their life is filled with darkness. Some of it is of their own making. Others live in circumstances where there is no light, no hope. They need to catch a glimpse of the hope in your life, and they will be drawn to that ultimate Light.

James wrote his letter to believers scattered abroad. They had a great opportunity to make an impact for Christ and the Gospel, but James had a word of warning for them:

But don't just listen to God's word. You must do what it says. Otherwise, you are only fooling yourselves.

JAMES 1:22 NLT

So today—let your LIFE shine before those around you so that they will see Jesus.

DAY THIRTY-SEVEN

He maketh me to lie down...

Many of us learned the 23rd Psalm in the King James language. Sometimes, the antiquated words and form get in the way of the passage's meaning. But other times, there is a lyrical quality that enhances and underscores the beauty and power of the psalm in deep ways.

"He maketh me to lie down in green pastures." That gives a different emphasis than the New Living Translation's "He lets me rest in green meadows." Sometimes, for our good, the Lord "maketh" us to lie down.

This came to my mind recently after returning from my second international trip in about three weeks. I was worn out and dealing with a pesky cough. The only remedy I had was to stay down for a few days. I needed to be refreshed. To be honest, that is not my nature. There is always something more to do, some planning and preparation, some writing, some something on my agenda. But God has something else for us than just "doing." Scripture reminds us, "...times of refreshment will come from the presence of the Lord, and he will again send you Jesus, your appointed Messiah." (Acts 19:20 NLT)

He maketh me to lie down...

The Old Testament makes a big deal of the Sabbath day of rest. The Lord went so far as to tell His people to give the land a time of rest, to be renourished and replenished. Is there a lesson for us in that? God has admonished us to "Be still and know that I am God." (Psalm 46:10 NLT)

From my recent experience, God has given me some new insights and vision for ministry. The Lord has reminded me of the nature of our world and the deep need for us to do as Peter says, to "...set Christ apart as Lord in your hearts and always be ready to give an answer to anyone who asks about the hope you possess." (1 Peter 3:15 NET)

I am reminded that along with the global opportunities we have to reach the unreached who have never heard the Gospel, we need to be aware of those right around us. Family, friends, the waiter at the restaurant, and the person on the airplane next to us. Be ready.

For me, it starts with refreshment. Rest. I should do that on my own before the Lord "maketh" me do it. But I also need to recognize that God is doing this for my good. And—for His great purpose.

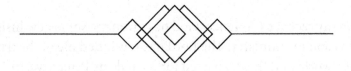

DAY THIRTY-EIGHT
That pesky law of Newton's!

You probably learned it in high school.

> Objects in motion tend to stay in motion.
> Objects at rest tend to stay at rest.

The second part of Newton's Law of Motion is the pesky one for me. When I'm in a warm bed on a cold day, I "tend" to stay at rest—under the covers. When I'm taking a hot shower, the hard thing is turning off the soothing water. I "tend" to want to just stay there, enjoying the warmth.

Guess what? This law also applies to us in leadership and in life. We can easily get stuck at rest, in our comfort zone, tending to stay there when we should be moving forward. We are "warm and safe" there. No risk. No issue with failure.

"A ship is always safe at shore, but that is not what it's built for."

I love that quote, which has been attributed to many, from author John A. Shedd to Albert Einstein to Navy admirals. It speaks to us on several levels.

It is easy to stay in our comfort zone to avoid facing challenges and the potential for failure. But little is accomplished by staying in our safe harbor. Someone has said, "While staying in our comfort zones might be safe and easy, it prevents us from fulfilling our true potential and purpose, which often requires taking risks and facing challenges."

God gives us a strong nudge to step out and fulfill our purpose. James' words are a call to action, not safety:

But don't just listen to God's word. You must do what it says. Otherwise, you are only fooling yourselves.

JAMES 1:22 NLT

When we get comfortable, we begin to fool ourselves. We become content with where we are and don't want to push out for fear of storms, challenges, or even failure. God calls us to be better than that.

We should embrace the great potential for growth and success that lies beyond our comfort zone. Set sail, face the challenges and opportunities, and know the Lord is with you as you step out. Above all, don't allow Newton's law to keep you from fulfilling God's assignment for you and those you lead. Don't stay at rest in your comfort zone. That's not what you were designed to do.

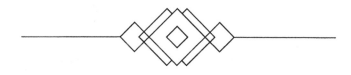

DAY THIRTY-NINE

Is there an "uncomfortable" zone?

We often talk about our "comfort" zone, the place where we feel… well…comfortable. That's not a bad thing. I want to be comfortable at home, around friends, and with our many global ministry partners. But is there a limit to our desire for comfort? Should there be an "uncomfortable" zone in our lives?

Have you ever worn shoes that were uncomfortable? I have. But that's not what I am talking about. There are times when our comfort zone is a deep pit that keeps us from seeing what the Lord wants us to see. Often, we build the walls of that pit so high that we can't see over our personal likes and spiritual prejudices. If you are saying "Ouch," don't feel too bad. Some of Jesus' closest disciples had built up such walls, and the Lord Jesus had to reorient them to His thinking.

You probably remember the account that happened after Jesus' death, resurrection, and ascension to heaven. The disciples were busy sharing the Good News, but in a way, they were stuck behind walls. They needed to learn the greatness of God's heart, and it happened through Peter.

In Acts 10, we find the account of Peter on the roof of Simon the Tanner's home. He had been there for a long time doing the Lord's amazing work of healing lives and even raising from the dead a young lady named Tabitha. While on the roof, Peter, in a dream-like state, saw something like a sheet being lowered. It was filled with all sorts of animals, birds, and even reptiles. When the voice from heaven instructed Peter to get up, kill, and eat them, Peter ran back into his comfort zone.

"Lord, I've never done that! Our Jewish laws have instructed me to not eat unclean things. Nope. Not doing it."

Then the voice from heaven built a bridge from Peter's comfort zone to God's plan for sharing the Good News.

> *"Do not call something unclean if God has made it clean."*
>
> ACTS 10:15 NLT

Peter's thoughts weren't bad or selfish. He was doing what he thought honored God. But the Lord needed to show Peter that the Gospel had a broader path, and it included the Gentiles.

I'm so glad Peter was willing to move out of his comfort zone to share the hope of Christ with that Roman soldier Cornelius. It opened the door for you and me to know the joy of salvation through Jesus Christ.

In my global travels, I have been confronted with things that are beyond my personal preferences and biblical understanding. I must be reminded that God's ways are not necessarily my ways. I have had to hear that voice that said, "Don't call something unclean that God has called clean." And I have had to adjust my understanding to the Lord's heart for the world.

There are certain things I won't adjust —the main tenets of our faith. But there are other practices and areas that are okay spiritually, even if they are different from what I have always known or thought.

So, how do you discern these things? I'm glad you asked! Prayer. The daily study of God's Word. An openness to the Holy Spirit's instruction that may take me out of my comfort zone, but place me where the Lord can do amazing things in the lives of others. I'm willing to be uncomfortable if it furthers the work and the spread of God's Good News to a lost and dying world.

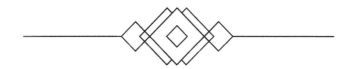

DAY FORTY

What matters to you?

It's just a little yellow sticky note with a quote on it. It's been sitting on my various computers for almost twenty years. I've moved it each time I upgraded my computer—so much so that the "sticky" part doesn't work, so I tape it on the computer where I can see it again and again. What is the quote?

> There is nothing more dangerous than a small character in a big assignment.

It's from my spiritual mentor, the late Henry Blackaby. I keep it to remind me that God honors character in our lives. But it goes even further. It is often said that character and integrity boil down to doing the right thing when no one else is watching. Jesus reminds us that those actions won't remain secret forever.

For all that is secret will eventually be brought into the open, and everything that is concealed will be brought to light and made known to all.

Luke 8:17 NLT

We are seeing that played out in news stories again and again, and it is damaging to the cause of Christ and for our culture.

The legendary basketball coach John Wooden drew a comparison between character and reputation. It's a good reminder.

"Be more concerned with your character than your reputation, because your character is what you really are, while your reputation is merely what others think you are."

Episcopal clergyman Phillips Brooks, the author of the Christmas song "O Little Town of Bethlehem," helped us understand how to build character—one brick at a time. He said, "Character may be manifested in the great moments, but it is made in the small ones."

It is in those quiet, alone moments that we are tempted to do the things that will eat away at our character. Eve was alone with the serpent when she took that fatal bite. The Lord was not around when Adam followed suit. Those "alone times" are the very times we need to guard ourselves. Our character is at stake. And, as with Adam and Eve, the repercussions can be devastating.

Is there a simple definition for the character of a person? For the believer, it is this: Christ-likeness. Listen to this from Oswald Chambers:

> "The expression of Christian character is not good doing, but God-likeness. If the Spirit of God has transformed you within, you will exhibit Divine characteristics in your life, not good human characteristics."

My friend Mike Huckabee wrote a book many years ago when the topic of character was being bantered about in the political realm. The title says much—Character IS the Issue.

It should be the issue for us in Christian leadership and in our daily lives. Make character—your character—matter. And strive to let your character reflect the character of the One who set the example for us, Jesus.

Dr. Ron Harris has been in media for six decades, with most of that time spent in Christian media. Coming to Christ at an early age, Ron sensed God leading him to serve the Lord through media beginning in his teenage years.

Through radio, television, teaching, and mentoring, Dr. Harris has touched lives worldwide for Christ and the Gospel. He founded MEDIA Alliance International in 2013 to strengthen the work of Christian media globally. The ministry now works with key leaders in over forty-five countries on five continents.

Dr. Harris is the author of *The Voice Behind You*, a memoir of his life led by God's voice. Ron and his wife Judy have been married for over 57 years.

All proceeds for the sale of this book go to MEDIA Alliance International to further the proclamation of the Gospel around the globe.

Additional copies of this devotional as well as Dr. Ron Harris' memoirs are available at mediaalliance.net/books.

Donations to the ministry can be made at mediaalliance.net/donations, or by check to MEDIA Alliance International, PO Box 200552, Arlington, TX 76006.

Made in the USA
Middletown, DE
20 January 2025